YOUR recipe could appear in our next cookbook!

Share your tried & true family favorites with us instantly at

www.gooseberrypatch.com

If you'd rather jot 'em down by hand, just mail this form to...

Gooseberry Patch • Cookbooks – Call for Recipes
PO Box 812 • Columbus, OH 43216-0812

If your recipe is selected for a book, you'll receive a FREE copy!

Please share only your original recipes or those that you have made your own over the years.

Recipe Name:

Number of Servings:

Any fond memories about this recipe? Special touches you like to add or handy shortcuts?

Ingredients (include specific measurements):

Instructions (continue on back if needed):

Special Code: **cookbookspage**

Over ➚

Extra space for recipe if needed:

Tell us about yourself...

Your complete contact information is needed so that we can send you your FREE cookbook, if your recipe is published. Phone numbers and email addresses are kept private and will only be used if we have questions about your recipe.

Name:
Address:
City: State: Zip:
Email:
Daytime Phone:

Thank you! Vickie & Jo Ann

Fall Cooking
with
Family & Friends

Good food and good friends...all the delicious flavors of fall, in over 200 easy recipes.

Gooseberry Patch

An imprint of Globe Pequot
246 Goose Lane
Guilford, CT 06437

www.gooseberrypatch.com

1•800•854•6673

Copyright 2022, Gooseberry Patch 978-1-62093-464-7

Do you have a tried & true recipe...

tip, craft or memory that you'd like to see featured in
a **Gooseberry Patch** cookbook? Visit our website at
www.gooseberrypatch.com and follow the
easy steps to submit your favorite family recipe.
Or send them to us at:

Gooseberry Patch
PO Box 812
Columbus, OH 43216-0812

Don't forget to include the number of servings your recipe makes,
plus your name, address, phone number and email address. If we
select your recipe, your name will appear right along with it...
and you'll receive a **FREE** copy of the book!

Contents

Dedication

*For everyone who treasures gathering with family
& friends for savoring fall colors, cheering on the
home team, watching the kids trick-or-treating
and sharing Thanksgiving dinner together.*

Appreciation

*We're grateful to all of you who shared your
most special recipes for fall.*

Pumpkin Patch
Memories

Fall Cooking
with Family & Friends

Autumn Memories

Carolyn Tellers
Erie, PA

Autumn has always been my favorite season. Some of my fondest memories involve rolling into piles of leaves at the bottom of my grandparents' hill, going for fall rides to pick out the perfect pumpkin and stopping at the local cider mills. Wonderful smells filled the air at my grandparents' houses and at home. One of my favorite treats was Grandma's homemade apple strudel. On Halloween, my brother, sister and I loved dressing up, especially in costumes Mom made for us. We had such fun going around the neighborhood and coming home to spread our goodies on the rug on the living room floor. On Thanksgiving, we would go hiking with relatives at nearby Presque Isle State Park, hoping to catch a glimpse of wild turkeys. We'd have a noon meal at Grandma and Grandpa's house, and a dinner at Grandy and Papa's house. I'm very grateful to have such a wonderful family, and grateful for all the fond memories!

There is music in the meadows,
in the air...autumn is here.
–William Stanley Braithwaite

Pumpkin Patch
Memories

Fall in the Ozarks

Pam Massey
Marshall, AR

Growing up in a small Ozark community here in Arkansas meant many changes. As school was back in session, the days turned cooler and the daylight hours shortened, our chores also changed. Some of my earliest memories include going with my grandparents to cut wood for keeping our homes warm. They loaded up five grandkids and a jug of water into Pawpaw's 3/4-ton truck, and off we'd go. We played until he had a tree down and cut up enough for us to load into the truck. We always had fun even while working, they always made all that work fun with picnics to share, letting us get dirty and playing with the dogs or calves. We never argued or refused to help. I never realized that it was work... just thought it was another adventure with the people I loved with all my heart.

Annual Leaf-Raking Party

Rhonda Schlarb
Muskego, WI

We are blessed to live on a property in Muskego, Wisconsin where we have 300-year-old oak trees. But as I always say, "If you like trees, you have to like leaves!" Each fall, just before it's time to turn our clocks (fall back!) we'd host our annual leaf-raking party. We'd invite the family out, with rakes in hand, to pitch in with the raking. They came with the promise of being fed a hot bowl of chili (red or white bean chicken) and some kind of apple dessert, as well as hot apple cider or hot chocolate. Always a great way to turn work into fun!

Fall Cooking
with Family & Friends

Daddy & the Colorful Leaves
Patricia Taylor
Louisville, KY

The tall oak and sugar maple leaves were dropping colorful gifts in our backyard. Christmas was around the corner and I was 10 years old. My father offered me money to help him in the backyard and earn some Christmas money, so I could buy my parents and sister gifts for Christmas. He would come in from work and rake leaves in the backyard. I remember Daddy's flannel shirts and baseball cap. I had such a good time raking the leaves in a pile, almost competing with Daddy. I would hold the bags open while he placed the leaves into the bags. As we finished, it almost became a game of who would finish first. The air was so crisp and the ground was damp, but the leaves were a blanket all around us as the moon came out on a cool autumn evening.

A Clean Sweep
Charlene McCain
Bakersfield, CA

Some of my fondest memories are of my two boys frolicking in the huge raked piles of leaves in our front yard. It was always as much fun to watch as it was to play. Most of the yards in our neighborhood were full of leaves just like ours was, except for one neighbor across the street who very happily did not have any trees. One year a big windstorm came to town. We knew it would blow down the rest of all our leaves, and were resigned to a big clean-up job. What a surprise next morning when we saw this tremendous wind had swept all of the neighborhood's leaves into the one yard without any trees! It had made a clean sweep for sure!

Pumpkin Patch Memories

Rolling in the Leaves

Sophia Collins
McHenry, MS

In my younger years, I lived in Hendersonville, North Carolina. My brother and I would play outside all day, rolling in the leaves. It was cold, so we were all bundled up, and the neighbors' chimneys would have smoke coming out from their fireplaces. We would rake all the leaves to the bottom of our backyard, then roll down into them. Mom would make us hot cocoa and bring it outside to us while we played. Every year, when it starts to cool down and I smell wood burning, I am transported back to that simple time, when life was all about playing outside, rolling in the leaves.

Pumpkins, Apples & Cider, Oh My!

Lora Eddings
Fort Walton Beach, FL

When our daughter was young and my mom was still with us, our fall tradition was to go to Shaw's Farm to pick out our pumpkins and fall decorations. We'd take a hayride through the farm, then get our pumpkins and treats. Then we would go to Rouster's Apple House. There we would get a variety of apples for the best apple pies, a gallon of cider that was so refreshing and the special cider popsicles! Sweet, sweet memories. Mom and Rouster's are no longer with us, but the memories are precious treasures of our hearts.

Delicious autumn! My very soul is wedded to it.
–George Eliot

Fall Cooking
with *Family & Friends*

Chili Sauce Day

Janis Parr
Ontario, Canada

As a small child and right into my teen years, I remember Mom and Dad making chili sauce together in the kitchen of our big old farmhouse, just before autumn arrived. The aroma from this spicy sauce filled the house. Dad grew the biggest, juiciest tomatoes in his garden and took great pleasure in picking only the best ones for the chili sauce. I can still see my parents in my mind's eye...Dad sitting at the kitchen table, carefully and patiently slicing and chopping the tomatoes, onions, peppers and celery and placing them in separate little piles, and Mom in her house dress and bib apron standing at the stove, slowly stirring and occasionally tasting the simmering sauce. When it came time to add the spices, both joined in at the stove, to sample the sauce and make sure that it was seasoned just right. Lovingly working together, they made jar after jar of the most delicious chili sauce to share with everyone, as well as cherished memories that I will always treasure.

I'm so glad I live in a world where there are Octobers.
–L.M. Montgomery

Pumpkin Patch Memories

Needle in a Haystack

Wanda Wilson
Hamilton, GA

Some years ago, my friend and I opened The Farmhouse, a gifts & antiques shop and restaurant down a secluded dirt road in Georgia. One of our favorite fall memories was our annual Scarecrow Contest. We provided the straw and old clothes for kids of all ages to create their funniest crow-scarers. One lady was particularly thrilled that she and her children won first place, until she arrived home and noticed that her wedding ring was no longer on her finger. After her call, we frantically took her scarecrow apart and actually found the proverbial "needle in a haystack"...her beautiful diamond ring. Their $100 prize money would not have gone far toward replacing that gorgeous, expensive ring! We were so thrilled that we could add another happy-ever-after ending to the memories of her ring.

A Perfect Fall Day

Carolyn Gulley
Cumberland Gap, TN

After our boys got married and left home, my husband and I looked for new things to do together. One fall, a nearby small community was having a fall festival and we decided to go. The festival was amazing, with street vendors selling antiques, crafts and food, and the shops along the downtown area were open with fall items displayed. We had so much fun! The weather was perfect and a few leaves were falling as we walked down the sidewalks. We purchased an antique red metal chair that day and I took a picture of my husband carrying it to the car. Now, years later we have returned each year to that festival. Some years we bought things and some years we didn't. But each time I see that red chair or that picture, I think about that first festival and the fun we had on that perfect fall day.

Fall Cooking
with Family & Friends

Halloween Night

Debra Arch
Kewanee, IL

Halloween night was always a fun memory for our family. Early in the day, I would start cooking apples harvested from our tree in a large slow cooker. Once they had cooked down to chunky applesauce, I would add sugar and a handful of cinnamon red-hot candies for one of our family's favorite desserts, candied applesauce! Its delicious smell spilled out the open door when greeting trick-or-treaters, filling the air with the sweet, warm scent of autumn! For dinner, I always prepared homemade chili and kept it warm in another slow cooker while the kids were off with Dad visiting family & friends to trick-or-treat. I stayed home to hand out mini candy bars and my special crispy rice pumpkins, tinted orange with food coloring mixed into the melted marshmallows, and decorated with candy corn eyes and teeth. Many nights were cold with a rainy mist...a perfectly spooky night! But once in awhile, the weather would be warm and balmy and the children didn't need coats to go over their costumes. I would have the back door open to greet the trick-or-treaters. I loved hearing the rustle of dried leaves as kids excitedly chattered and giggled their way to my house! Our kids are all grown now, but I still make the crispy rice pumpkins and take them to fall wiener roasts and other autumn gatherings.

On Halloween, the thing you must do
Is pretend that nothing can frighten you
And if something scares you and you want to run
Just let on like it's Halloween fun!
–19th-century Halloween postcard

Pumpkin Patch **Memories**

Halloween at Grandma's House

Stephanie Kemp
Lakeville, OH

Grandma always made Halloween special at her house. My two siblings, three cousins and I would go to Grandma's house for supper that night. She usually had pizza, chips and other goodies that we all loved. Then we would put on our homemade costumes and go out to gather our goodies from the neighborhood. At the end of the night, we would come back to Grandma's house and knock on the door. She always had a special bag of our favorites especially for each of us, so one by one, we would see what goodies she had for us. Then we all went into her house and traded the candy that we had collected with each other. It was a great time, and Grandma enjoyed it so much as well. When we all had our own children and Grandma turned into a great-grandma, she continued the fun with them. It was fun to get together with our cousins as adults and replay our childhood. Oh, the fun that we had and the stories we have to tell over the good times with Grandma!

Halloween Memories

Cherry Flynn
Mount Sterling, IL

Years ago, I started having an annual Halloween party at my house for my younger sister and my two best friends. I go all-out with the decorations, and each year the tablescape changes. Everyone pitches in with the food and most of the time it is Halloween-themed also. It is a great time for all of us to get together to catch up on each other's lives. There's usually lots of laughter, sometimes tears, but mostly fun and good times with wonderful people who are an important part of my life!

Fall Cooking
with *Family & Friends*

Homemade is Best

Stephanie O'Connor
Ontario, Canada

When I was growing up, we didn't have a lot of money. With three kids to get ready for Halloween, my parents always got us excited weeks before, preparing our costumes. We always made them and helped our parents construct them. We went trick-or-treating with our neighbors and we consistently won prizes for our costumes! But the most fun was the family time spent making our vision come to life. My favorite costume to date has to be the year I went as a TV journalist, with a "television" surrounding my upper body! We got so many compliments from everyone, including a large group of teens who thought it was so cool to see a Zenith TV walking around! To this day, my motto is still, "homemade is best."

Halloween Fun

Rebecca Frey
Prescott Valley, AZ

I grew up in a small town in Michigan. Every year at Halloween, our school had a costume contest on the athletic field for all the grades. Afterwards, we got cider and doughnuts, the best I can ever remember. Then we would finish the night off with trick-or-treating in town. It was such great fun as a kid! Then the next day, we would play in the fallen leaves, building houses out of them and talking about the candy we'd gotten the night before. I have many more fond memories of my little hometown in the fall, but these are some of my favorites.

Pumpkin Patch
Memories

Back to School, Parents' Night

Andrea Czarniecki
Northville, MI

I was a teacher for 31 years and loved my job! Each fall, I would get a new class list and got my classroom ready for a new year. I loved to make the room as bright and interesting as could be. In September, I always created an outline of each student's body on paper. They would spend several hours coloring and decorating the cut-outs of themselves. We would tape the cut-outs in their seats for Parents' Night. The kids loved to see if their parents could "find" them in their new seats.

Fall Family Memories

Betty Kozlowski
Newnan, GA

Growing up in New Orleans, the summers were long and humid, so when fall weather came, we loved being outside enjoying the cooler weather. One of the photos in my family album shows me (in junior high) and my two older sisters (in high school), wearing plaid shirts and jeans, roller skating in front of our house. The sidewalks were in good shape, and we had an added bonus...a long, wide driveway that went all the way to the back of the house. We spent many happy hours enjoying the fall weather and flying along on our skates!

School bells are ringing loud and clear;
Vacation's over, school is here.
–Winifred C. Marshal

Fall Cooking
with *Family & Friends*

An Autumn Drive

Joan Raven
Cicero, NY

Every autumn season, my husband faithfully takes out my autumn and Halloween totes. They're overstuffed with decorations for our home that we've collected through many memorable years of our marriage and family. We always take a weekend to take a drive and savor the colors and scents this beautiful season surrounds us with. Of course, before we leave, a tried & true Gooseberry Patch slow-cooker recipe is prepared. Upon our return home, the aroma is there to warmly greet us, as well as our grandchildren asking, "Where did you go? What did you see on your adventure today?" Ahh...an amazing annual autumn drive and an awesome Gooseberry Patch dinner awaiting. Yes, we welcome the autumn season in all its splendor. Thank you, Mother Nature! Thank you, Gooseberry Patch! Thank you, dear husband, for our annual autumn drive memories!

I can see the woods in their autumn dress, the oaks purple, the hickories washed with gold, the maples and the sumacs luminous with crimson fires...

–Mark Twain

Pumpkin Patch **Memories**

Halloween Baby Surprise

Kathy Grashoff
Fort Wayne, IN

My third son was born one year on October 3, but we still had two older boys who wanted to go trick-or-treating at the end of the month. It was a beautiful Halloween that year, but cold. I did not want to miss out, even though my husband said he'd take out the boys. I had a bigger coat that my sister had given me, so I strapped little Andrew on my chest and zipped that coat right up around him. Voilà! Andrew and I got to enjoy that night with the family. All the neighbors asked what I'd done with the baby, so I unzipped the coat for them to take a peek! Andrew is now in his late 30s, but I still have that memory of his first Halloween.

Falling Leaves

Theresa Esposito
Freehold, NJ

One of my favorite memories of fall was when my children were little. We had been out going to garage sales, which we enjoyed doing on Saturday mornings. We had gone to this one house, and parked across the street. When we were walking back to the car, we saw a little field with a beautiful tree that had bright yellow leaves. There was a breeze, and all the leaves were raining down onto the green grass. My two children, who were probably three and five at the time, started dancing around under the leaves. They loved it! Seeing them expressing their joy at the beauty of the falling leaves was wonderful to watch, and it is still one of my favorite fall memories to this day.

Fall Cooking
with Family & Friends

Thankful for
Autumn Majesty

Tracie Carlson
Richardson, TX

The memory of a brisk Thanksgiving morning years ago in
Pennsylvania is still fresh on my mind. It was our first Thanksgiving
in Pennsylvania. I was in awe of the gorgeous array of fall foliage
which displayed a striking contrast to the early morning mist hovering
above the pond, just a stone's throw from our living room. I had a
strong cup of hot coffee in hand, savoring a few moments of early
morning beauty before getting ready to prepare the big Thanksgiving
feast. Then I noticed something moving in the trees, maybe a branch,
or possibly one of the many deer that Bucks County had in great
abundance. I squinted for a moment, trying to make out what was
clearly a rustling in the leaves, coming closer to the pond. First I made
out one of the biggest racks I've ever seen, and then the most majestic
buck ever. He stood proudly for a minute or two. How lucky was I to
take in such a magnificent sight, on Thanksgiving Day no less, I
thought to myself. I called to my husband, who got within viewing
range just in time to see the buck leap back into the woods,
disappearing into the rich hues of gold, orange and vibrant red.

Pumpkin Patch
Memories

Groundhogs Making Coffee *Priscilla Howard*
Morehead, KY

Growing up in eastern Kentucky in the foothills of Appalachia, almost every morning you could expect fog creeping up out of the hills and hollers. It was a majestic misty fog, and my dad would always say while driving down the road, "Groundhogs are making coffee again this morning." I heard this from my dad starting at a very young age, and truly believed it for years! I could just imagine groundhogs sitting around the base of an old poplar tree, brewing their morning coffee, and the mist from the brewing pots rising into the air. The years have gone by now, and I try to use this old expression as often as possible, to as many new people I can. There is just something about this picture which makes me feel warm and magical!

Two sounds of autumn are unmistakable...the hurrying rustle
of crisp leaves blown along the street...by a gusty wind,
and the gabble of a flock of migrating geese.

–Hal Borland

Fall Cooking
with Family & Friends

Holiday Cooking

Lisa Showers
Mount Penn, PA

As a mother, you hold some things dear to your heart. My fondest memories are of our Thanksgiving dinners. I would spend the week before Thanksgiving baking pastries for the holiday, 15 different desserts to make sure everyone had their favorite, along with traditional ones and some new ideas. The night before Thanksgiving is when it all starts to happen. The oven is on non-stop as the turkey and ham are prepared, filling the house with the aroma of heavenly scents. The kids are excited waiting for the big day with their mouths watering, waiting to taste the wonderful food. Roast turkey and baked ham, homemade stuffing, mashed and sweet potatoes, vegetables of all kinds, blueberry muffins, bread, rolls, cranberry relish...all shared with friends and relatives. As we get older, people pass and time goes by, we always have our memories of Thanksgiving days together to hold close and cherish.

What we're really talking about is a wonderful day set aside on
the fourth Thursday of November when no one diets.
I mean, why else would they call it Thanksgiving?

–Erma Bombeck

Pumpkin Patch **Memories**

Thanksgiving at Grandma & Grandpa's

Becky Bosen
Syracuse, UT

One of my fondest memories of growing up is of Thanksgiving dinners at my grandmother and grandfather's house. The two-bedroom house was tiny, but always full to the brim on holidays. The smell of roast turkey and gravy, stuffing and of course pumpkin pie permeated every nook and cranny of that little house. Filled with the wonderful scents of the season and the laughter of aunts, uncles and cousins, memories were made and are still cherished today.

Love of Autumn

Helen McKay
Edmond, OK

When I was growing up, the autumn season was spent harvesting our garden and orchards, then helping my mom can and freeze all the wonderful vegetables and fruits. It was a time of raking pile after pile of fallen leaves, then jumping into them or making leaf houses. It was a timc of drives up into the mountains looking at the beautiful leaves that had changed into colors of reds, oranges and golds. Walking through the groves of aspen trees with golden leaves showering down around us. The chilly nights and cooler days. I love autumn...my favorite season!

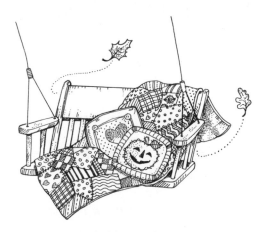

Fall Cooking
with *Family & Friends*

Friendship & Autumn Theme Parties

Ernestine Trent
Elkview, WV

One of my favorite memories is from when we lived in Shiloh, Illinois on Stonebridge Drive. We had such sweet neighbors and made close friends with a few of the families. Our neighbor and friend Patricia loved to host theme parties for our "Stonebridge Gang." One autumn, my husband and Patricia both grew sunflowers...it was a friendly competition. So for the party, we had a special judge come to declare the sunflower champion! We spent many crisp fall days sitting around the fire pit, enjoying good food and great conversations. We didn't realize how precious those memories would become. We have since moved back home to West Virginia, but will never forget the family we made from a group of strangers.

Kindergarten Pumpkin Patch

Monica Britt
Fairdale, WV

There's not much that's more exciting than taking your kindergarten class on a field trip to the pumpkin patch! Every autumn I'm reminded of those sweet memories. The event would always start with a hayride, then the kids would run through the pumpkin patch selecting just the right pumpkin. After visiting the farm animals and running through the corn maze, the kids would eat a delicious picnic lunch while chatting about all the wonderful things they had experienced. So many memories were always made!

All seasons are beautiful for the person who carries happiness within.
–Horace Friess

Fall Breakfast
Favorites

Fall Cooking
with Family & Friends

Sunrise Bake

Teri Johnson
Montezuma, IA

When you have a houseful of guests, this is a great breakfast recipe to fix ahead of time! Wake them up with the wonderful aroma.

1 lb. pork breakfast sausage
    links
8 eggs, beaten
2 c. evaporated milk
1/2 t. onion powder
1/2 t. garlic powder

2 c. favorite shredded cheese
1 c. green, red or yellow pepper,
    chopped
2 green onions, sliced
8 slices bread, cut into
    1/2-inch cubes

In a skillet over medium heat, cook sausage links until browned on all sides; drain. Meanwhile, in a large bowl, combine remaining ingredients except bread cubes; stir until well mixed. Slice sausages and fold into egg mixture; gently stir in bread. Spoon mixture into a greased 13"x9" baking pan. Bake, uncovered, at 350 degrees for 45 minutes, or until set and lightly golden. Serve warm. Makes 8 servings.

Make the most of a sunny autumn morning...take breakfast outdoors! Toss a quilt over the table and serve some warm muffins with homemade jam and fresh fruit.

French Toast Muffins

Judy Couto
Kerman, CA

My mom used to make these muffins, way back when. They are always loved by little ones. For a little extra sweetness, fold in 1/2 cup golden raisins.

1-1/2 c. all-purpose flour
3.4-oz. pkg. instant vanilla
   pudding mix
2 t. baking powder
1/4 t. salt
1-1/4 t. cinnamon, divided
2 eggs, divided

1-1/4 c. milk, divided
3/4 c. plus 2 T. brown sugar,
   packed and divided
3 slices white bread, cut into
   1/2-inch cubes
1/2 c. butter, melted
2 T. maple syrup

In a large bowl, combine flour, dry pudding mix, baking powder, salt and one teaspoon cinnamon; set aside. In a separate bowl, whisk together one egg, 1/4 cup milk, 2 tablespoons brown sugar and remaining cinnamon. Add bread cubes; stir until moistened and set aside. In another bowl, whisk together remaining egg, milk and brown sugar. Stir in melted butter; add to flour mixture and stir just until moistened. Batter will be lumpy. Spoon batter into 10 to 12 muffin cups sprayed with non-stick vegetable spray. Top with bread mixture; press lightly into batter with spoon. Bake at 350 degrees for 26 to 28 minutes, until a toothpick inserted in the center tests clean. Brush warm muffins with syrup; let cool in pan for 5 minutes. Remove to a wire rack; cool slightly before serving. Makes about one dozen.

Such a neighborly gesture! Invite your child's new school friend and her family over for a weekend brunch. Send them home with a basket filled with brochures and coupons for local shops and attractions.

Fall Cooking
with Family & Friends

Dad's Breakfast Pizza

Kimberly Trotter
Monroe, MI

My father used to make this delicious recipe for my mom, my sister and me. It brings back fond memories of the times we spent around the table as a family enjoying my dad's handiwork in the kitchen. When we got older, he passed on his knowledge and expertise in the kitchen to my sister and me.

1 doz. eggs
1/4 c. milk
salt and pepper to taste
2 14-1/2 oz. cans diced tomatoes
   with green chiles, drained
1-1/2 c. shredded Colby Jack
   cheese

1 green pepper, diced
1 onion, diced
1/2 lb. mushrooms, diced
Optional: cooked sausage, ham
   or bacon, sliced jalapeño
   peppers

Combine eggs, milk, salt and pepper in a blender; process until smooth. Pour into a 13"x9" baking pan sprayed with non-stick vegetable spray. Bake, uncovered, at 350 degrees for 10 minutes; remove from oven. Meanwhile, rinse out blender; add both cans of tomatoes with juice to blender and process until smooth. Pour tomatoes over egg mixture. Layer with cheese, vegetables and optional ingredients, if desired. Return to oven for another 10 minutes, or until eggs are set. Cut into squares to serve. Makes 12 servings.

Tickle the kids with Jack-o'-Lantern oranges at breakfast. Slice the tops off navel oranges and scoop out the pulp with a spoon. Draw on silly or spooky faces with food coloring markers. Spoon in fruit salad and serve...clever!

Fall Breakfast
Favorites

Bran Muffins

Hailey Farrar
San Luis Obispo, CA

When chilly weather sets in, these are the perfect addition to breakfast! The recipe makes a lot, but can easily be cut in half. You can also bake a few at a time and return the batter to the fridge, so you can have hot muffins each morning.

4 eggs, beaten
4 c. buttermilk
5 t. baking soda
2 t. salt
2 c. sugar

1 c. margarine, melted and
    slightly cooled
5 c. all-purpose flour
15-oz. pkg. bran & raisin cereal
1 c. raisins

In a large bowl, combine all ingredients except flour, cereal and raisins. Mix well; fold in remaining ingredients. Cover and refrigerate for 48 hours. Spoon batter into greased muffin cups, filling 2/3 full. Bake at 400 degrees for 15 to 20 minutes. Makes 4 dozen.

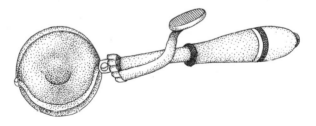

Use an old-fashioned ice cream scoop to fill muffin cups
with batter...no drips, no spills and muffins turn out
perfectly sized.

Fall Cooking
with *Family & Friends*

Puffy Pumpkin French Toast
Marsha Baker
Pioneer, OH

I revised a recipe for classic French toast to make it pumpkin-flavored.
It's puffy from the addition of flour and perfect for fall.

1 c. all-purpose flour
2 t. baking powder
1 T. brown sugar, packed
2 eggs, beaten
1 c. milk
1 t. vanilla extract
1 t. pumpkin pie spice

1/3 to 1/2 c. canned pumpkin
oil for frying
10 to 12 slices frozen Texas
    toast, or any day-old
    thick-sliced bread
Garnish: maple syrup or
    powdered sugar

In a small bowl, combine flour, baking powder and sugar; mix well and set aside. In a large bowl, whisk together eggs, milk and vanilla; set aside. In a cup, blend spice into pumpkin; stir well and whisk into egg mixture. Add flour mixture to egg mixture; whisk until blended. Batter may have a few lumps. Heat a non-stick skillet over medium-high heat; add enough oil to barely cover the bottom. Dip one side of each bread slice into batter; flip it over and cover the other side with batter. Let any extra batter drip off; add to hot skillet. Cook for 4 to 5 minutes on each side, until golden. Serve dusted with powdered sugar or drizzled with maple syrup. Serves 5 to 6, 2 slices each.

Whip up a luscious topping to dollop on waffles and pancakes...yum!
Combine 3/4 cup whipping cream, 2 tablespoons cream cheese and
one tablespoon powdered sugar. Beat with an electric mixer on
medium speed until soft peaks form. Spoon into a small crock
and keep refrigerated.

Fall Breakfast Favorites

Brown Sugar Cinnamon Waffles

Melanie Lowe
Dover, DE

On a chilly morning, breakfast doesn't get much better than this!
Treat everyone...top waffles with a dollop of whipped cream.

1-3/4 c. buttermilk	2 t. baking powder
1/2 c. butter, melted and cooled	1 t. baking soda
2 eggs, beaten	1 t. salt
1-3/4 to 2 c. all-purpose flour	1-1/2 t. cinnamon
2 T. light brown sugar, packed	Garnish: butter, maple syrup

In a large bowl, whisk together buttermilk, melted butter and eggs; set aside. In another large bowl, whisk together 1-3/4 cups flour and remaining ingredients. Add to buttermilk mixture and whisk until just smooth; add remaining flour if too thin. Let batter stand about 5 minutes. Preheat a waffle iron over medium-high heat; spray with non-stick vegetable spray. Add 1/3 cup batter per waffle to waffle iron; bake according to manufacturer's directions. Garnish as desired. Makes 8 waffles.

Make breakfast waffle sandwiches for a delicious change.
Tuck scrambled eggs, a browned sausage patty and
a slice of cheese between waffles...yum!

Fall Cooking
with *Family & Friends*

Thanksgiving Weekend Brunch Bake

Jackie Smulski
Lyons, IL

My late father, Ed, loved his turkey leftovers. This dish was perfect for Sunday brunch after Thanksgiving.

2-1/2 to 3 c. leftover cooked
   stuffing
2 c. leftover cooked turkey,
   cubed
1/2 bunch green onions,
   thinly sliced

1 red pepper, finely chopped
6 eggs, beaten
1-1/2 c. milk
1/3 c. mayonnaise
salt and pepper to taste

In a greased 8"x8" baking pan, layer stuffing, turkey, green onions and red pepper; set aside. In a large bowl, whisk together eggs, milk and mayonnaise until blended; spoon over mixture in pan. Season with salt and pepper. Bake, uncovered, at 350 degrees for 65 to 75 minutes, until a knife tip inserted near center comes out clean. Let stand 10 to 15 minutes before serving. Serves 4 to 6.

Deep-Dish Coffee Cake

Sandy Coffey
Cincinnati, OH

My relatives love this coffee cake! It's great for visitors as a quick & easy breakfast served with coffee, tea or orange juice.

18-1/2 oz. pkg. yellow cake mix
1/2 c. butter, melted
4 eggs, divided
8-oz. pkg. cream cheese,
   softened

16-oz. pkg. powdered sugar,
   divided

In a large bowl, combine dry cake mix, butter and 2 unbeaten eggs; mix well. Spread in a greased and floured deep 13"x9" baking pan; set aside. Combine remaining eggs, cream cheese and powdered sugar, reserving a small amount of powdered sugar for garnish. Beat well and spread over batter in pan. Bake at 350 degrees for 40 to 45 minutes. Cool slightly; sprinkle with reserved powdered sugar and cut into squares. Serves 10.

Fall Breakfast Favorites

Apple Fritters

Margaret Welder
Madrid, IA

Apples have always held a special place in my heart, as my parents once had an apple farm. This recipe was a favorite treat with my kids for a special breakfast. Here's an easy tip, if you have a set of round cookie cutters in different sizes like I do. Slice the apples horizontally, then use the cutters to peel and core the slices.

1 c. all-purpose flour
2 T. sugar
1 t. baking powder
1/2 t. salt
2 eggs, beaten

2/3 c. milk
3 T. oil, divided
4 apples, peeled, cored and
    sliced into rings
Garnish: powdered sugar

In a large bowl, whisk together flour, sugar, baking powder and salt; set aside. In another bowl, whisk together eggs, milk and one tablespoon oil; add to flour mixture and stir to form a batter. Heat remaining oil in a skillet over medium heat until hot. Dip apple rings into batter; add to skillet. Cook as you would a pancake, turning as they turn golden. Sprinkle with powdered sugar to serve. Serves 6.

Start off a tailgating Saturday right...invite friends to join you for breakfast! Keep it simple with a breakfast casserole, baskets of muffins and a fresh fruit salad on the menu. It's all about food and friends!

Fall Cooking
with Family & Friends

Doug's Favorite Fruit Salad

Janet Sharp
Milford, OH

My husband loves fruit salad, so I started putting this combination of fruits together. Now he doesn't want any other fruit salad! This salad is great for breakfast.

15-1/4 oz. can sliced peaches, diced
15-oz. can mandarin oranges
1/2 c. maraschino cherries, sliced, drained and 2 T. juice reserved
2 c. strawberries, hulled and sliced or chunked

1/2 fresh pineapple, peeled and cut into chunks
2 kiwi, halved and sliced
1 mango, peeled, pitted and diced
Optional: 1 c. mini marshmallows

In a large bowl, combine peaches with juice, oranges with juice and remaining ingredients; mix gently. Cover and chill in refrigerator overnight. Makes 8 to 10 servings.

Want a warm, sweet treat on a busy morning? Cinnamon toast is ready in a jiffy. Spread softened butter generously on one side of toasted bread, sprinkle with cinnamon-sugar and broil until hot and bubbly, one to 2 minutes. Perfect with a mug of hot cocoa!

Fall Breakfast
Favorites

Lala's Cinnamon Rolls

Kayla Herring
Hartwell, GA

My sister found this recipe one day while scrolling the internet. The first time she made them, they were a hit! This is our family's first choice when getting together for breakfast. It pairs perfectly with coffee and your favorite breakfast casserole.

12-oz. pkg. Hawaiian sweet rolls,
   halved horizontally
1/2 c. butter, softened
1/4 c. brown sugar, packed

1 T. cinnamon
1/2 c. powdered sugar
2 to 3 t. milk

Arrange bottom halves of rolls in a lightly greased 13"x9" baking pan and set aside. In a small bowl, mix butter, brown sugar and cinnamon; spread half of mixture evenly over rolls. Add top halves of rolls; spread with remaining butter mixture. Bake, uncovered, at 350 degrees for 12 to 13 minutes. Stir together powdered sugar and milk; drizzle over rolls. Makes one dozen.

Monkey Bread

Rosemary Lightbown
Wakefield, RI

A favorite recipe from a childhood friend. You can also add chopped nuts or dried fruit...yummy!

3 7-1/2 oz. tubes refrigerated
   buttermilk biscuits
2 t. cinnamon

1/2 c. sugar
1/2 c. butter, sliced
1 c. brown sugar, packed

Cut biscuits into quarters; set aside. Combine cinnamon and sugar in a shallow bowl. Roll biscuits in cinnamon-sugar; arrange in a well-greased Bundt® pan. Melt butter in a small saucepan over low heat; add brown sugar. Cook and stir until mixture comes to a boil; spoon over biscuits in pan. Bake at 350 degrees for 30 minutes. Immediately invert onto a serving dish. Serves 8 to 10.

Spicy Cheesy Grits

Crystal Shook
Catawba, NC

The whole family will love these grits, not just for breakfast but at suppertime too! Be sure to use quick-cooking grits, not instant. If you like, some diced, cooked bacon, sausage or ham may be added.

4 c. chicken broth
1/4 t. salt
1 c. quick-cooking grits,
   uncooked
1 c. shredded sharp Cheddar
   cheese, divided
1/2 c. shredded Pepper
   Jack cheese

2 T. butter, sliced
1/2 t. garlic powder
10-oz. can diced tomatoes with
   green chiles
2 eggs

In a large saucepan, bring chicken broth and salt to a boil over medium heat. Add grits, stirring constantly until blended; cook over low heat for 5 minutes. Stir in 1/2 cup Cheddar cheese, Pepper Jack cheese, butter, garlic powder and tomatoes with chiles. Cook and stir until cheese is melted and blended together; set aside. Beat eggs in a small bowl; add a small amount of grits to eggs and mix well. Gradually add egg mixture to grits in pan; stir until combined. Pour into an 8"x8" baking pan sprayed with non-stick vegetable spray. Bake, uncovered, at 350 degrees for 30 minutes. Top with remaining cheese; bake for additional 10 minutes, or until cheese is melted. Makes 4 to 6 servings.

There are so many fun harvest festivals, antique sales and county fairs every autumn...be sure to visit at least one! A hearty breakfast together with family & friends will start the day off right.

Fall Breakfast Favorites

Apple Pie Breakfast Bake

Mel Chencharick
Julian, PA

This recipe is a scrumptious brunch treat! Or top with
ice cream and caramel syrup for a fantastic dessert.

2 11-oz. tubes refrigerated
  French bread dough
1 c. butter, melted
21-oz. can apple pie filling
14-oz. can sweetened
  condensed milk

1 t. apple pie spice
1 t. vanilla extract
1 c. pure maple syrup, warmed

Place both loaves of dough seam-side down on a greased baking sheet,
side by side. Cut 4 diagonal slashes in each loaf with a sharp knife.
Bake at 350 degrees for 26 to 30 minutes, until deeply golden. Cool for
20 minutes. Cut loaves into 1/2-inch cubes to measure 7-1/2 cups; set
aside. (Half of one loaf may be left; reserve for another use.) Spread
melted butter in a lightly greased 13"x9" glass baking pan; evenly layer
pie filling and bread cubes in pan. In a bowl, stir together condensed
milk, spice and vanilla until well blended. Spoon over bread, gently
pressing bread down to absorb milk. Bake, uncovered, at 375 degrees
for 25 to 35 minutes, until bubbly and deeply golden. Let stand for
15 minutes. Serve warm with maple syrup. Serves 8.

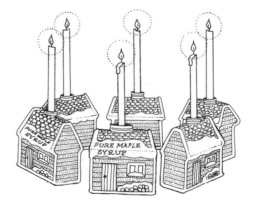

Cabin-shaped maple syrup tins make whimsical candleholders
for the breakfast table. Tuck tapers into the openings and
arrange in a group.

Fall Cooking
with Family & Friends

Gravy & Biscuits in One

Joan Chance
Houston, TX

My daughter loved gravy over biscuits for breakfast. This is a fast & easy recipe...just add fresh fruit and serve.

1 lb. ground pork sausage
1/4 c. butter, sliced
1/3 c. all-purpose flour
3-1/2 c. whole milk

1/4 t. salt
1/2 t. pepper
7-1/2 oz. tube refrigerated
    biscuits

Brown sausage in a cast-iron skillet over medium heat, stirring often, about 6 minutes. Transfer sausage to a paper towel-lined plate to drain. Drain skillet and wipe clean with a paper towel. Reduce heat to low and add butter to skillet; cook until melted. Whisk in flour until smooth. Cook, whisking constantly, for one minute. Gradually whisk in milk. Increase heat to medium, and cook, whisking constantly, until thickened and bubbly, 10 to 12 minutes. Stir in browned sausage, salt and pepper. Arrange 8 to 9 biscuits in a circle on top of sausage mixture, leaving about 1/2 inch around edge of skillet. Place one biscuit in the center. Bake, uncovered, at 350 degrees for 20 to 25 minutes, until biscuits are golden and gravy is bubbly. Let stand 10 minutes before serving. Serves 8 to 10.

A sweet keepsake for a family brunch. Copy one of Grandma's tried & true recipes onto a festive card, then punch a hole in the corner and tie the card to a rolled napkin with a length of ribbon.

Eggs with Tortilla Chips

Vickie
Gooseberry Patch

This is a Spanish breakfast dish called "Migas" meaning crumbs, referring to the broken tortilla chips. It's a fun and tasty way to make breakfast for overnight guests...use up those leftover party chips & salsa from the night before!

10 eggs, beaten
2 T. milk
salt and pepper to taste
1-1/2 T. butter
1 c. shredded Mexican-blend
    cheese

3/4 c. favorite salsa, partially
    drained
1 c. tortilla chips, crushed
Optional: additional salsa

In a large bowl, whisk together eggs, milk, salt and pepper; set aside. Melt butter in a large skillet over medium heat. Pour egg mixture into pan. Cook to desired doneness, stirring occasionally, about 4 to 5 minutes. Top with cheese just before eggs are set. Fold in salsa and crushed chips. Serve with additional salsa, if desired. Makes 4 to 6 servings.

Poached eggs in a jiffy! Add a tablespoon of water to each muffin cup and break an egg into the cup. Bake at 350 degrees, 11 to 13 minutes for runny yolks, a little longer for firmer yolks. Remove from oven. Let stand for one minute before removing eggs with a slotted spoon. Serve with toast, or as you like.

Fall Cooking
with *Family & Friends*

Monte Cristo Breakfast Bake
Courtney Stultz
Weir, KS

I don't get to enjoy a tasty Monte Cristo sandwich very often, but it's one of my favorites. When I thought of creating this breakfast dish, I wasn't sure how it would all come together. Turns out, it's much easier to make than the sandwich and it's a crowd favorite for brunch! For an extra twist, use slices of cinnamon-raisin bread.

10 slices bread, cubed
1/4 c. butter, melted
1 T. Dijon mustard
1/4 c. deli baked ham, cubed
1/4 c. deli roast turkey, cubed
1 c. Swiss cheese, shredded or
 diced

10 eggs, beaten
1 c. whipping cream
1/3 c. raspberry preserves
Garnish: powdered sugar

Spread bread cubes in a lightly greased 13"x9" baking pan; set aside. In a small bowl, stir together melted butter and mustard; drizzle over bread cubes. Top bread with ham, turkey and Swiss cheese; set aside. In another bowl, whisk together eggs and cream. Pour egg mixture over bread mixture. Bake, uncovered, at 350 degrees for about 35 to 45 minutes, until golden and eggs are set. In a cup, stir preserves until smooth; drizzle over top. Sprinkle with powdered sugar. Serves 8.

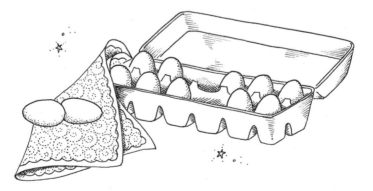

Fresh eggs can safely be kept refrigerated for 4 to 5 weeks,
so go ahead and stock up when they're on sale.

Fall Breakfast Favorites

Apple-Nut Coffee Cake

Sheryl Bohm
Derby, KS

This recipe was passed down from my parents. The recipe is in my mom's handwriting, but my dad is the one who makes this moist, tender cake.

1/2 c. butter, softened
1 c. sugar
2 eggs, beaten
1 t. vanilla extract
2-1/2 c. all-purpose flour

1 t. baking powder
1 t. baking soda
1/4 t. salt
1 c. sour cream
2 c. apples, cored and diced

In a large bowl, blend butter and sugar. Add eggs and vanilla; stir well and set aside. In another bowl, sift flour, baking powder, baking soda and salt. Add flour mixture to butter mixture alternately with sour cream, mixing well. Fold in apples. Spread batter in a greased 12"x9" baking pan. Sprinkle Nut Topping over batter. Bake at 350 degrees for 35 minutes. Cut into squares. Serves 12.

Nut Topping:

1/2 c. chopped walnuts or pecans
1/2 c. brown sugar, packed

2 T. butter, melted
1 t. cinnamon

Combine all ingredients; mix well.

Honey butter is delicious on warm muffins and toast.
Simply blend 1/2 cup each of honey and softened butter.

Fall Cooking
with *Family & Friends*

Ham & Cheese Oven Omelet
Connie Giardina
Binghamton, NY

A no-fuss way to make a delicious omelet.

6 eggs
1/4 c. fat-free milk
1/8 t. salt
1/8 t. pepper

1/8 t. garlic powder
3/4 c cooked ham, diced
1-1/4 c. shredded Cheddar
   cheese, divided

Spray a 9" pie plate with non-stick vegetable spray. Place pie plate in oven set to 400 degrees. In a bowl, beat eggs until frothy. Stir in milk, seasonings, ham and one cup cheese. Remove pie plate from oven; pour egg mixture into pie plate. Set pie plate in center of oven. Bake at 400 degrees for about 20 minutes, until puffed and set in center. Sprinkle with remaining cheese; let stand until melted. Cut into 4 wedges and serve. Serves 4.

Smoked Salmon & Dill Spread
Melanie Taynor
Everett, WA

Delish on toasted bagels! Mom found this recipe in an ad years ago, and we've enjoyed it ever since.

8-oz. pkg. cream cheese,
   softened
1/2 c. smoked salmon, chopped

1 T. fresh dill weed, chopped,
   or 1 t. dried dill weed

In a bowl, beat cream cheese until smooth. Fold in salmon and dill weed. Cover and chill about for one hour before serving. Makes 1-1/4 cups.

Egg dishes are a perfect way to use up tasty tidbits from the fridge...bacon, ham, chopped veggies and cheese. Warm quickly in a skillet and set aside for an omelet filling, or scramble the eggs right in.

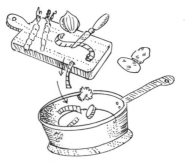

Seasoning for Fried & Scrambled Eggs

Eileen Bennett
Jenison, MI

This tasty seasoning is such a family favorite, I always double the recipe. It has many uses, but my favorite is using it to season egg dishes. Scott, my oldest grandson, always has to have this on his corn on the cob.

1 T. celery seed	2 t. paprika
1 t. dried parsley	1 t. garlic powder
1 c. sea salt or salt substitute	1 t. chili powder
2 T. onion powder	1/2 t. cayenne pepper

Using a spice grinder, grind celery seed and parsley well. Transfer to a bowl; add remaining ingredients. Mix all together using a whisk. Store in an airtight container. To use, fill a shaker-top spice jar with mixture. Will keep for many weeks. Makes 1-1/3 cups.

Make your own country-style breakfast sausage, seasoned just as you like. To one pound ground pork, add one teaspoon ground sage, 3/4 teaspoon salt, 3/4 teaspoon pepper and 1/4 teaspoon brown sugar. A dash or two of cayenne pepper can be added too.

Honey-Walnut Breakfast Loaves

Bev Traxler
British Columbia, Canada

I make this gem every time the kids come to visit. They love it... everyone does! I generally make four loaves at a time, because it freezes very well.

small amounts shortening
  and flour
18-1/2 oz. pkg. yellow, golden
  or French vanilla cake mix
3 eggs, beaten

1 c. water
1/3 c. butter, melted
1/4 c. honey
1 c. chopped walnuts or pecans,
  divided

Grease the bottoms of two 9"x5" loaf pans with shortening; sprinkle lightly with flour and set aside. In a large bowl, combine dry cake mix, eggs, water, butter, honey and 1/2 cup nuts. Beat with an electric mixer on low speed for 30 seconds. Increase speed to medium and beat for 2 minutes. Divide batter evenly between pans. Bake at 350 degrees for 40 to 45 minutes, until a toothpick inserted in center comes out clean. Cool in pans for 10 minutes. Run a knife around sides of pans to loosen loaves; remove from pans. Cool completely. Spread Vanilla Glaze over top, allowing some to drizzle down the sides. Sprinkle with remaining nuts. Makes 2 loaves, 8 slices each.

Vanilla Glaze:

1 c. powdered sugar
1/2 t. vanilla extract

1 to 2 T. milk, divided

Stir powdered sugar, vanilla and one tablespoon milk until well mixed. Stir in additional milk, one teaspoon at a time, until smooth.

To freeze: Place completely cooled, glazed loaves on a baking sheet; place in freezer until set. Wrap loaves and return to freezer.

Fall Breakfast Favorites

Homemade Pumpkin Butter

Tina Vawter
Sheridan, IN

*Whip this up in a jiffy and spoon into a canning jar...just add
a bow for a great hostess gift! Great with homemade
pumpkin bread, zucchini bread or banana bread.*

1 c. butter, softened
1/4 c. canned pumpkin
2 T. brown sugar, packed
2 T. honey

1 t. cinnamon
1/4 t. nutmeg
1/8 t. ground cloves
salt to taste

In a bowl, beat butter with an electric mixer on medium-low speed until
light and fluffy. Add remaining ingredients; beat until combined. Keep
refrigerated in a covered container. Makes 1-1/2 cups.

Autumn is a terrific time to get outdoors. Place a hook by the
back door and keep a favorite comfy sweater on it. You never
know when you'll want to run outside to see the colorful
leaves or a harvest moon.

Fall Cooking
with *Family & Friends*

Country Pancakes & Waffles

Joy Dyck
Manitoba, Canada

I created this recipe one afternoon while trying to decide what to make for supper. Everyone knows breakfast is better at suppertime! Jazz it up by adding some berries, chocolate chips, cinnamon...you name it, it works.

1 c. all-purpose flour	1 c. milk
1 T. baking powder	1 T. honey
1/2 t. salt	1 egg, beaten
2 T. butter	1 t. vanilla extract

In a large bowl, whisk together flour, baking powder and salt; set aside. Melt butter in a microwave-safe bowl. Add milk and honey; microwave until warm. Pour butter mixture into flour mixture and stir until smooth; stir in egg and vanilla. Let batter stand while preheating a greased pancake griddle. Add batter, about 1/2 cup per pancake. Cook over medium-low heat until bubbles appear all over the surface; turn and cook other side. For waffles, add 3/4 to one cup batter per waffle to a greased preheated waffle iron. Cook according to manufacturer's directions. Serves 2.

Whip up some special hot cocoa with a round disc of
Mexican chocolate...it has cinnamon and sugar already mixed in!
Bring 4 cups milk almost to a boil, add the chocolate and
whisk until it's melted and creamy.

Fall Breakfast Favorites

Apple, Pear & Cranberry Sauce

Arlene Smulski
Lyons, IL

With an abundance of fresh fruits, this is delicious spooned over pancakes or waffles for a weekend breakfast. It could also be served as a side at Thanksgiving dinner.

2 T. butter
2 Gala or Honey Crisp apples,
   cored and chopped
1 Bartlett pear, cored and
   chopped
1-1/2 t. fresh thyme, snipped

2/3 c. cranberries, thawed
   if frozen
1 T. light brown sugar, packed
1/2 t. vanilla extract
2 t. cider vinegar

Melt butter in a large skillet over medium heat. Add apples, pear and thyme. Cook, stirring occasionally, until fruit begins to soften, about 3 to 4 minutes. Add cranberries, brown sugar and vanilla. Cook until apples and pear begin to lightly caramelize, stirring occasionally, for 2 to 3 minutes. Remove from heat; stir in vinegar. Serve warm. Makes 4 servings.

Make school-day breakfasts fun! Cut the centers from a slice of toast with a cookie cutter, serve milk or juice with twisty straws or put a smiley face on a bagel using raisins and cream cheese.

Fall Cooking
with *Family & Friends*

Scrambled Eggs for a Crowd
Liz Blackstone
Racine, WI

One day, my son signed me up to make breakfast for the whole football team! What to do, what to do? These eggs baked up easily while I fixed bacon and hashbrowns for the boys. Success!

1/3 to 1/2 c. butter, melted
2 doz. eggs, beaten
1-1/2 t. salt

pepper to taste
1-1/4 c. half-and-half
1-1/4 c. whole milk

Pour melted butter into a 13"x9" glass baking pan coated with non-stick vegetable spray; set aside. In a large bowl, whisk eggs and seasonings until smooth and well blended. Gradually whisk in half-and-half and milk; pour into pan. Set pan on lowest oven rack. Bake, uncovered, at 350 degrees for 10 minutes. Remove pan from oven; stir eggs gently and return to oven. Bake another 15 to 20 minutes, until eggs are just set. Let stand several minutes; eggs will finish cooking once removed from oven. Serve immediately. Makes 10 to 12 servings.

Alongside a covered dish of scrambled eggs, set out warmed tortillas, shredded cheese, salsa and sliced avocado. Guests will be able to fix their own breakfast burritos, just the way they like!

Fall Breakfast **Favorites**

Breakfast Potatoes with Bacon & Onion

Wendy Jo Minotte
Duluth, MN

Using baked potatoes left over from dinner, this quick and filling breakfast cooks up very quickly. I use kitchen scissors to cut the bacon right into the skillet. Serve with scrambled eggs and fresh-squeezed orange juice.

6 to 8 baked potatoes
1 lb. bacon, cut into
   1/2-inch pieces

1 c. onion, diced
salt and pepper to taste

Peel and dice potatoes; set aside. In a large non-stick skillet, cook bacon over medium heat until beginning to brown. Add onion; cook until soft and golden. Add potatoes, stirring to blend. Cover and cook until golden and heated through, about 10 minutes, stirring occasionally. Season with salt and pepper. Serves 6 generously.

Caramel-Hazelnut Cafe Mocha

Robin Hill
Rochester, NY

A special hot beverage that's welcome any time of day.

2 qts. half-and-half
1/2 c. chocolate hazelnut spread
1/2 c. caramel topping
1/4 c. baking cocoa

2 T. instant espresso coffee
   powder
Garnish: whipped cream,
   additional caramel topping

In a 4-quart slow cooker, whisk together all ingredients except garnish. Cover and cook on low setting for 5 to 6 hours, whisking once or twice during cooking. Whisk again; ladle into mugs and garnish as desired. Makes 12 servings.

Fall Cooking
with *Family & Friends*

Apple Butter Muffins

Geraldine Weedman
Caldwell, ID

I found this recipe years ago in a magazine. When I want a snack or something to go with my coffee in the morning, it is quick to make and the muffins are delicious. Sometimes instead of putting the apple butter in the center, I just mix 1/2 cup to 3/4 cup of apple butter into the batter. It is good either way.

1-3/4 c. all-purpose flour
1/3 c. plus 3 T. sugar, divided
2 t. baking powder
1/4 t. salt
1/2 t. cinnamon
1/4 t. nutmeg
1/8 t. allspice

1/8 t. ground ginger
1 egg, lightly beaten
3/4 c. milk
1/4 c. oil
1/2 c. thick apple butter
1/2 c. chopped pecans

In a large bowl, combine flour, 1/3 cup sugar, baking powder, salt and spices; set aside. In another bowl, combine egg, milk and oil; stir into flour mixture just until moistened. Fill greased or paper-lined muffin cups with one rounded tablespoon of batter. Top each with a rounded teaspoon of apple butter; add a little more batter to cover apple butter. Combine pecans and remaining sugar; sprinkle over muffins. Bake at 400 degrees for 15 to 18 minutes. Cool muffins in pan for 10 minutes; remove to a wire rack. Makes one dozen.

Make an easy fabric liner for a basket of freshly baked muffins. Use pinking shears to cut an 18-inch square of cotton fabric in a perky fall print. Pretty on the breakfast table...great for gift baskets!

Fall Breakfast Favorites

Slow-Cooker Steel-Cut Apple Oats

Selma Hannen
Cypress, TX

*Enjoy this warm, hearty oatmeal as is, or set out containers of
brown sugar and cream by the crock for everyone to add.*

1 c. steel cut-oats, uncooked
4 c. water
2 Honey Crisp apples, cored and
    thinly sliced

15-oz. can cream of coconut
2 T. sugar
1-1/2 t. cinnamon
1/8 t. nutmeg

Combine all ingredients in a 5-quart slow cooker; stir to mix well. Cover
and cook on low setting for 8 hours or overnight. Makes 8 servings.

Mix up some autumn potpourri. Combine nature-walk finds like
seed pods and nuts with whole cloves, allspice berries and cinnamon
sticks from the kitchen spice rack. Toss with a little cinnamon
essential oil and place in a decorative bowl.

Fall Cooking
with *Family & Friends*

Kielbasa Quiche

Melissa Flasck
Rochester Hills, MI

These hearty quiches can be served as breakfast, lunch or dinner. I like to make them two at a time. The hashbrowns can be thawed overnight in the fridge, or on the counter for 30 minutes before making.

2 c. frozen diced hashbrowns,
    thawed
3 T. butter, softened
2 t. seasoned salt, divided
3 eggs, beaten

3 c. milk
1/2 t. smoked paprika
1/2 c. shredded Cheddar cheese
1/2 c. Kielbasa sausage, chopped

Combine hashbrowns, butter and one teaspoon seasoned salt in an ungreased 9" pie plate. Press mixture down into plate, covering the bottom and any extra going up the sides of plate. Bake, uncovered, at 350 degrees for 20 minutes. Meanwhile, in a bowl, whisk together eggs, milk, remaining salt and paprika; fold in cheese. When hashbrown crust is removed from oven, spoon sausage evenly over hashbrowns. Pour egg mixture into crust, covering hashbrowns and sausage. Bake at 350 degrees for 30 minutes, or until set. Cool slightly; cut into wedges. Serves 5.

When you rise in the morning, form a resolution to
make the day a happy one for a fellow creature.
–Sydney Smith

Fall Breakfast Favorites

Cheddar-Bacon Apple Bake
Virginia Campbell
Clifton Forge, VA

This recipe was a team effort, with family members naming their favorite ingredients to put together as a new way to serve apples. It tastes wonderful, and the aroma has everyone up and gathered together at the breakfast table! A mix of tart & sweet, green, yellow & red apples is scrumptious, and there's no need to peel them.

8 c. apples, cored and chopped
1 c. sugar
3/4 c. self-rising flour
1/8 t. nutmeg
2 c. shredded sharp
   Cheddar cheese

6 slices bacon, crisply cooked
   and crumbled
1/2 c. butter, melted

Spread apples in a greased 13"x9" baking pan; set aside. In a bowl, stir together sugar, flour, nutmeg, cheese and crumbled bacon. Blend in melted butter; sprinkle mixture evenly over apples. Bake, uncovered, at 350 degrees for 30 minutes, or until golden. Serves 10 to 12.

For delicious baked apple recipes, some of the best varieties
are Granny Smith, Gala and Jonathan as well as old-timers
like Rome Beauty, Northern Spy and Winesap. Mix a few
different kinds for extra flavor.

Fall Cooking
with *Family & Friends*

Lemon Sweet Roll Cake

*Nina Jones
Springfield, OH*

*The citrusy flavor of this cake goes well with rich breakfast foods.
I like to top it with an extra dollop of lemon pie filling...yum!*

1-1/2 c. all-purpose flour
1/2 c. sugar
1/8 t. salt
2 t. baking powder
3/4 c. milk

1 egg, beaten
2 t. vanilla extract
1/4 c. butter, melted
1 c. lemon pie filling

In a large bowl, combine flour, sugar, salt and baking powder; mix well and set aside. In a small bowl, whisk together milk, egg and vanilla. With an electric mixer on low speed, gradually add milk mixture to flour mixture; beat until well combined. Gradually pour in melted butter; beat until combined. Pour batter into a greased 8"x8" baking pan. Dot pie filling over batter by spoonfuls. With a knife, swirl pie filling down into batter. Bake at 350 degrees for 30 to 35 minutes. Remove from oven; cool slightly. Pour Glaze over cake. Let stand for about 10 minutes, until glaze sets up. Cut into squares; serve warm or at room temperature. Serves 12.

Glaze:

1 c. powdered sugar
juice of 1/2 lemon

3 T. milk

Mix together all ingredients, adding enough milk for a smooth consistency.

During the first week of school, deliver a tray of your favorite breakfast goodies to the teachers' lounge...it's sure to be appreciated!

Warm & Cozy
Soups & Breads

Fall Cooking
with *Family & Friends*

Chilly-Day Meatball Soup

Nicole Pinkosh
Columbia Heights, MN

I enjoy making this slow-cooker soup on chilly fall and winter evenings for my family & friends. My favorite memory is eating this soup around a bonfire after a lovely walk in the woods.

22-oz. pkg. frozen Italian-style
   meatballs
16-oz. pkg. frozen peas & carrots
2 14-oz. cans beef broth
19-oz. can tomato-basil soup
2-1/2 c. water

3 T. garlic, minced, or to taste
1/2 c. onion, finely diced
1 T. Italian seasoning
salt and pepper to taste
12-oz. pkg. tri-color penne
   pasta, uncooked

In a 6-quart slow cooker, combine all ingredients except pasta; stir gently. Cover and cook on high setting for 4 hours. About 20 minutes before serving time, cook pasta according to package directions; drain. To serve, add desired amount of pasta to serving bowls; ladle soup over pasta. Serves 4 to 6.

Sprinkle the inside of your Jack-o'-Lantern with some pumpkin pie spice. When the candle is lit, it will smell delicious!

Vegetable Cheese Soup

Melissa Bromen
Marshall, MN

This cheesy vegetable-filled soup will warm you to your toes!

4 c. water
4 cubes chicken bouillon
1 c. celery, chopped
1 c. onion, chopped
2-1/2 c. potatoes, peeled
    and cubed
1 c. carrots, peeled and sliced

10-oz. pkg. frozen mixed
    vegetables
2 10-3/4 oz. cans cream of
    chicken soup
1 to 1-1/2 c. milk
16-oz. pkg. pasteurized process
    cheese, cubed

In a soup pot over medium-high heat, combine water, bouillon, celery and onion. Cook for 20 minutes; do not drain. Add potatoes, carrots and frozen vegetables; reduce heat to medium. Cover and cook for 20 minutes. Uncover; add soup and desired amount of milk. Add cheese; cook and stir until cheese is melted and soup is heated through. Makes 6 to 8 servings.

Bread bowls make a hearty soup extra special. Cut the tops off round loaves of bread and hollow out, then rub with olive oil and garlic. Bake at 350 degrees for 8 to 10 minutes, until crusty and golden. Ladle in soup and enjoy!

Grandma's Hamburger Vegetable Soup

Susan McCoy
Dixon, IL

Easy and delicious! This recipe has been handed down for three generations, and fiddled with along the way. You can use whatever is in the pantry. Serve with warm cornbread and you've got a meal!

1 lb. lean ground beef
2 10-3/4 oz. cans tomato soup
1.1-oz. pkg. beefy onion
　　soup mix
2 c. water

15-oz. can peas
1 c. potatoes, peeled and cubed
1 c. carrots, peeled and sliced
1/4 c. long-cooking barley,
　　uncooked

Brown beef in a large stockpot or Dutch oven over medium heat; drain. Whisk together tomato soup, soup mix and water in a large bowl; add to beef. Add undrained peas, potatoes, carrots and barley. Cook over medium heat for at least one hour, stirring occasionally. May also combine browned beef and remaining ingredients in a 5-quart slow cooker; cover and cook on low setting for 4 to 6 hours. Serves 8.

Variation: Instead of potatoes, add 1/2 cup uncooked long-cooking rice or one cup uncooked elbow macaroni. Increase water by one cup; cook as directed.

Polka-dot pumpkins! Use acrylic paint to paint spots on pumpkins. Even faster...pick up some sheets of colorful round stickers at the office supply store to decorate pumpkins with!

Hearty Sausage Soup

Darla Cottom
Terre Haute, IN

My boys loved this slow-cooker soup when they were little. Use your own judgment on the amount of spaghetti, to make it as thick or as soupy or as you want. Caution...a little goes a long way!

1 lb. ground pork sausage
1 green pepper, diced
1 onion, diced
1/3 of a 16-oz. pkg. angel hair
    pasta, uncooked and broken
    into 2-inch pieces

28-oz. can diced tomatoes
14-1/2 oz. can diced tomatoes
12-oz. can tomato juice
garlic salt to taste
1/8 t. sugar

Brown sausage in a skillet over medium heat. Drain; transfer to a 5-quart slow cooker. Add green pepper and onion; place desired amount of spaghetti pieces on top of vegetables. Add tomatoes with juice and remaining ingredients. Cover and cook on low setting for 4 to 6 hours. Makes 6 to 8 servings.

Welcome chilly fall weather with a soup swap. Invite friends to bring labeled containers of their favorite soup, for example, 6 quarts each for 6 guests. Recipe cards would be a nice touch too. Set out spoons and samples of each for tasting, along with saltine crackers. After sampling, everyone gets to take home a quart of each. Tasty and fun!

Fall Cooking
with Family & Friends

Italian Pantry Soup

Joslyn Hornstrom
Elgin, IL

This hearty and satisfying soup recipe is the result of the pandemic of 2020, when I had only pantry and freezer supplies on hand. With a little imagination, we can all find comfort in our pantries and freezers during troubling times.

1 lb. ground mild Italian
   pork sausage
3 14-1/2 oz. cans chicken broth
14-1/2 oz. can petite diced
   tomatoes
15-oz. can diced potatoes
15.8-oz. can cannellini beans
10-oz. pkg. frozen chopped
   spinach, thawed and
   squeezed dry

1 t. onion powder
1 t. garlic powder
1/2 t. Italian seasoning
pepper to taste
Optional: 5-oz. can evaporated
   milk
Garnish: grated Parmesan cheese

Cook and crumble sausage in a large soup pot over medium heat; drain. Add broth, undrained tomatoes, potatoes and beans, spinach and seasonings; bring to a boil. Reduce heat to low; cover and simmer for 10 minutes. If a creamier soup is desired, stir in milk; heat through. Garnish servings with Parmesan cheese. Serves 8.

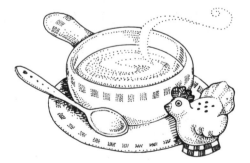

November 15 is National Clean-Out-Your-Refrigerator Day...cook up a big pot of "surprise soup" with whatever you find in the fridge! Perfect for a fall day, and the fridge will be all set for Thanksgiving groceries.

Reuben Soup

Katelinn Fite
Stout, OH

This is a very full-bodied soup that's great on cold weather days.
It's wonderful if you're feeling chilled or down with the flu.
Serve with warm rye bread or rolls.

1/2 c. butter
1 onion, diced
1 T. garlic powder, or to taste
4 c. chicken broth
2 c. whole milk
6 new redskin potatoes, cubed

2 8-oz. pkgs. cream cheese,
   cubed
28-oz. can sauerkraut, well
   drained and patted dry
8-oz. pkg. pepperoni or pastrami,
   diced

Melt butter in a soup pot over medium heat. Add onion and garlic powder; cook until onion is soft. Add chicken broth and milk; bring to a boil. Add potatoes and cook until fork-tender. Reduce heat to medium-low; stir in cream cheese and sauerkraut until smooth. Simmer until heated through. Sprinkle with pepperoni or pastrami and serve. Makes 6 servings.

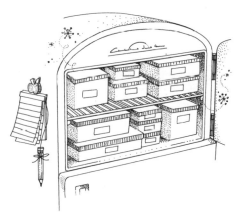

How comforting to have a freezer full of delicious soups! Make a double batch of a favorite soup, then transfer half to a freezer-safe container and freeze. To serve, thaw overnight in the fridge...heat until bubbly in a saucepan on the stovetop.

Fall Cooking
with *Family & Friends*

Pam's Pasta Fagioli

Pam Schremmer
Wichita, KS

I was trying to copy a soup that I love from a famous restaurant and came up with this one. I serve it with bread hot from the oven. It's easy and delicious!

8-oz. pkg. small shell pasta, uncooked
14-oz. pkg smoked pork sausage link, sliced, or 1 lb. ground beef, browned & drained
14-1/2 oz. can chicken broth
15-1/2 oz. can red kidney beans, drained and rinsed

15-oz. can tomato sauce
14-1/2 oz. can diced tomatoes
14-1/2 oz. can cut green beans
1/2 c. water
1 t. Cajun seasoning
1 t. dried, minced onions
Garnish: shredded Parmesan cheese

Cook pasta according to package directions; drain. Meanwhile, brown sausage or beef in a skillet over medium heat; drain. To pasta in pot, add sausage or beef and remaining ingredients except cheese. Bring to a boil over high heat. Reduce heat to medium-low and simmer for 20 minutes, stirring occasionally. Top with shredded cheese. Makes 6 servings.

Top soup bowls with crunchy cheese toasts...yum! Brush thin slices of French bread lightly with olive oil. Broil for 2 to 3 minutes, until golden; turn over. Sprinkle with shredded Parmesan cheese. Broil another 2 to 3 minutes, until cheese melts.

Warm & Cozy
Soups & Breads

Savory Muffins

Louise Graybiel
Ontario, Canada

These tasty muffins are very easy and go well with vegetable soup.

2 c. all-purpose flour
1 T. baking powder
2 t. sugar
1/2 t. salt
1 T. fresh chives, minced

3/4 c. shredded sharp
   Cheddar cheese
1 egg
1-1/4 c. milk
1/4 c. canola oil

In a large bowl, combine flour, baking powder, sugar and salt; mix in chives and cheese. In a separate bowl, beat egg, milk and oil. Stir egg mixture into flour mixture until moistened; batter should be a bit lumpy. Divide batter evenly into 12 greased or paper-lined muffin cups. Bake at 400 degrees for 20 to 25 minutes, until a toothpick inserted in the center comes out clean. Makes one dozen.

Bean & Potato Chowder

Carolyn Deckard
Bedford, IN

We enjoy this soup often on chilly autumn nights.

20-oz. pkg. refrigerated diced
   potatoes with onions
14-oz. can vegetable broth
1/3 c. all-purpose flour
1 c. shredded Swiss cheese

3 c. milk
1 t. Italian seasoning
15-1/2 oz. can navy beans,
   drained and rinsed
salt and pepper to taste

In a Dutch oven over medium-high heat, bring potatoes and vegetable broth to a boil. Reduce heat to medium-low; cover and simmer for 4 minutes. In a large bowl, toss together flour and cheese until cheese is coated; gradually stir in milk. Add milk mixture and Italian seasoning to potato mixture. Cook and stir over medium heat until thickened and bubbly. Stir in beans; cook and stir one minute more, or until heated through. Season with salt and pepper. Serves 4.

Salt pork adds old-fashioned flavor to pots of soup beans
and green beans. Look for it at the meat counter.

Ranch Chicken Chili

Emily Doody
Kentwood, MI

I got this slow-cooker recipe years ago at a freezer meal party hosted by a girlfriend. It became a family favorite and a real crowd-pleaser for get-togethers. I serve it with tortilla chips, sour cream, shredded cheese and salsa for topping...delicious!

1 to 1-1/2 lbs. boneless, skinless
　chicken breasts
15-1/2 oz. can black beans,
　drained and rinsed
15-1/2 oz. can Great Northern
　beans, drained and rinsed
14-1/2 oz. can diced tomatoes
　with green chiles

1 c. onion, finely diced
1 green pepper, finely diced
1 c. frozen corn
1 c. chicken broth
1-oz. pkg. ranch seasoning mix
1 T. taco seasoning mix
2 T. lime juice
8-oz. pkg. cream cheese, cubed

In a 6-quart slow cooker, combine all ingredients except cream cheese. Cover and cook on low setting for 8 hours. Shred chicken and add back into chili. Stir in cream cheese; cover and cook 30 more minutes. Stir to combine and serve. Makes 8 servings.

A hometown chili cook-off! Ask neighbors to bring a pot of their best "secret recipe" chili to share, then have a friendly judging for the best. You provide lots of crackers and cornbread, cool drinks and bright red bandannas for terrific lap-size napkins. Sure to be fun!

Warm & Cozy
Soups & Breads

Beef Barley Soup

Lisa Gowen
Saint Charles, MO

We love a good hearty beefy soup on a cool fall day or a cold winter day. This is a favorite! If you are like me and do not care for peas, use a combination of mixed vegetables that doesn't include peas, so that you enjoy every bite.

3/4 lb. lean stew beef, cut into
   1-inch cubes
1 T. oil
14-oz. can beef broth
1 c. onion, chopped
1 stalk celery, chopped
2 cloves garlic, minced

14-1/2 oz. can diced tomatoes
1 c. canned or frozen mixed
   vegetables, drained
2/3 c. quick-cooking barley,
   uncooked
salt and pepper to taste

In a large soup pot over medium heat, brown beef in hot oil. Drain; stir in beef broth, onion, celery and garlic. Bring to a boil; reduce heat to medium-low. Cover and simmer 1-1/2 hours, stirring occasionally. Stir in tomatoes with juice, vegetables and barley. Return to a boil; reduce heat to medium-low. Simmer, covered, for about 15 minutes, until vegetables and barley are tender. Makes 8 servings.

Festive croutons! Butter bread slices and cut into shapes using mini cookie cutters. Bake at 425 degrees for 6 to 7 minutes on each side, or until crisp and golden. Garnish filled soup bowls with croutons before serving.

Fall Cooking
with *Family & Friends*

Mucho Minestrone

Sonia Elmore
Canyon, TX

A perfect soup for a cool autumn day! Fast, easy preparation so you can be back on the sofa under a cozy blanket in a jiffy.

2 lbs. ground beef chuck
2 14-1/2 oz. cans diced tomatoes
   with green chiles
2 cans ranch-style beans
   or chili beans

2 19-oz. cans minestrone soup
2 T. sherry or water
2 T. butter, sliced
Garnish: sour cream

Brown beef in a large soup pot over medium heat; drain. Add undrained tomatoes, beans, soup and sherry or water; bring to a boil. Reduce heat to medium-low and simmer for 30 minutes. Add butter; simmer another 5 minutes. Serve topped with a dollop of sour cream. Makes 8 to 10 servings.

Chicken Curry Soup

Beverly Verdery
Normal, IL

Good for a quick, simple supper with friends, served with hot bread and a fruit salad.

1 c. celery, finely chopped
1/2 c. onion, finely chopped
2 T. butter
2 10-3/4 oz. cans cream of
   chicken soup

3 c. half-and-half or milk
1/2 t. curry powder, or more
   to taste
1/8 t. salt
Garnish: sliced toasted almonds

In a large saucepan over medium heat, sauté celery and onion in butter for 3 to 5 minutes. Add remaining ingredients except garnish; whisk until well blended. Heat through, but do not boil. Garnish servings with a sprinkle of almonds. Makes 4 to 6 servings.

The ornament of a house is the friends who frequent it.
–Ralph Waldo Emerson

Simple Potato Soup

Brittany Marsh
Madisonville, KY

This recipe was handed down to me from my mother. It's an easy way to feed the family and doesn't take long to make.

6 to 8 russet potatoes, peeled
  and cubed
10-3/4 oz. can cream of
  chicken soup
10-3/4 oz. can cream of
  mushroom soup
1-1/2 c. whole milk

8-oz. pkg. cream cheese,
  room temperature
1/4 c. butter, softened
salt and pepper to taste
Garnish: chopped fresh chives,
  crumbled bacon, shredded
  Cheddar cheese

Cover potatoes with water in a soup pot; bring to a boil over high heat. Cook until fork-tender; drain and return to pot. Meanwhile, in a separate saucepan, combine remaining ingredients except garnish and bring to a boil, whisking frequently. Add soup mixture to potatoes. Garnish with desired toppings. Makes 4 to 6 servings.

For a change, spice up Simple Potato Soup with crushed tortilla chips, shredded Pepper Jack cheese and chopped jalapeño peppers!

Fall Cooking
with *Family & Friends*

Green Enchilada Chicken Soup

Shirin Blackwell
Garden Ridge, TX

My husband loves this soup! It's super-easy to make, using rotisserie chicken. If you prefer, you can cook and shred 2 or 3 large chicken breasts instead of the rotisserie chicken. Just cook them in the broth before adding all the other ingredients. Super quick! Serve with warm tortillas.

1 sweet onion, diced
2 T. avocado or canola oil
2-1/2 lb. deli rotisserie chicken, boned and shredded
32-oz. container chicken broth
2 14-oz. cans green enchilada sauce
1 c. whipping cream
1/2 c. cream cheese, softened
1/2 c. salsa verde
2-1/2 c. shredded Monterey Pepper Jack cheese
salt and pepper to taste

In a large soup pot over medium heat, sauté onion in oil until translucent. Add remaining ingredients except salt and pepper. Cook over low heat until heated through and all cheeses are melted, stirring occasionally. Season with salt and pepper, as desired. Makes 8 servings.

Make some crunchy tortilla strips for a fun soup topping.
Cut tortillas into strips, then deep-fry quickly. Drain and
sprinkle over your favorite spicy soup.

Warm & Cozy
Soups & Breads

Best-Ever Southern Cornbread *Becky Butler*
Keller, TX

My whole adult life, I have been searching for the "best-ever" recipe for baked goods that I prepare often. This is the cornbread recipe I've made for 20 years! True Southern cornbread is not sweet, but if you like it sweet, 2 to 3 tablespoons of sugar can be added.

1 c. yellow cornmeal
1/2 c. all-purpose flour
1 t. baking powder
1/2 t. baking soda
1 t. salt

1-1/2 c. buttermilk
2 eggs, beaten
1/4 c. butter, bacon drippings
  or oil
Garnish: softened butter

Place a 10" cast-iron skillet in 425-degree oven to preheat. In a large bowl, whisk together cornmeal, flour, baking powder, baking soda and salt; set aside. In a small bowl, whisk together buttermilk and eggs. Add buttermilk mixture to cornmeal mixture and stir until just combined; some small lumps are all right. Carefully remove hot skillet from oven; brush with butter, drippings or oil. Pour batter into hot skillet and spread evenly. Bake at 425 degrees for 15 to 18 minutes, until a toothpick inserted into the center comes out clean. Turn cornbread out onto a dinner plate and cut into wedges, or cut into wedges and serve out of the hot skillet. Serve with softened butter. Makes 8 servings.

Still too warm for a fire? Give your fireplace a welcoming autumn glow...fill it with pots of flame-colored orange and yellow mums.

Fall Cooking
with *Family & Friends*

Ann's Crawfish Corn Soup

Ann Farris
Biscoe, AR

I love corn and I love crawfish, so I decided to put the two together in a delicious soup. It is best to make it the day before and let all the ingredients blend together. In the summertime, I use fresh corn off the cob and fresh crawfish tails.

1/2 c. butter
2 T. all-purpose flour
1 c. sweet onion, finely chopped
1/4 c. green onions, chopped
12-oz. pkg. frozen crawfish tails
2 15-1/4 oz. cans corn, drained
2 14-3/4 oz. cans cream-
   style corn
10-3/4 oz. can cream of
   mushroom soup
4 c. milk
1/2 c. shredded Cheddar cheese
1/2 t. Worcestershire sauce
salt and pepper to taste
Cajun white pepper seasoning
   to taste

In a large pot, melt butter over medium heat. Add flour to butter; cook and stir until blended. Add all onions and sauté until wilted. Add remaining ingredients; reduce heat to medium-low. Cook for 40 minutes, stirring often. Makes 6 servings.

Chowders and cream soups are perfect comfort foods. Make yours extra creamy and rich tasting...simply replace milk or water in the recipe with an equal amount of evaporated milk.

Oatmeal Batter Bread

Kathy De Schinckel
Davenport, IA

No kneading is required! You'll love this easy recipe.

3 c. all-purpose flour, divided
1 c. old-fashioned oats,
   uncooked
1/4 c. sugar
1 t. salt

1-1/4 oz. pkg. active dry yeast
1 c. milk
1/4 c. butter, sliced
2 eggs, beaten

In a large bowl, combine 1-1/2 cups flour, oats, sugar, salt and yeast; set aside. Combine milk and butter in a one-quart saucepan. Cook over medium heat, stirring occasionally, for about 2 to 4 minutes, until mixture reaches 120 to 130 degrees on a cooking thermometer. Add milk mixture and eggs to flour mixture. With an electric mixer on medium speed, beat for 3 minutes, or until well mixed. Stir in remaining flour; beat until smooth. Cover and let rise in a warm place until double in size, one to 1-1/2 hours. Stir down batter; spread in a greased 9"x5" loaf pan. Cover and let rise until double, 40 to 50 minutes. Bake at 375 degrees for 25 to 30 minutes, until loaf sounds hollow when tapped. Remove from pan; cool completely and slice. Makes one loaf.

Stock up on homemade jams and jellies at farmers' markets...
you can't have too many! Scrumptious with fresh-baked bread,
or add to a favorite dessert recipe. You can even add a cute fabric
topper to turn a jar of jam into a last-minute hostess gift.

Fall Cooking
with Family & Friends

Creamy Turkey Noodle Soup   Lisa Kastning
Marysville, WA

Years and years ago, while at a mutual friend's house, I met the sweet lady who gave me this recipe. When she gave it to me, she told me it would be the "best soup you'll ever eat," and she was so right. Unfortunately, it was the only time our paths ever crossed. If only I could tell her how many years my family and I have enjoyed it!

1 carcass from a 15-lb. roast
   turkey
5 qts. water
1 c. celery, chopped
1/2 c. celery leaves, chopped
1 c. onion, chopped
7 cubes chicken bouillon
1 T. salt
1/4 t. pepper
1 bay leaf

1 c. fresh or frozen peas
1 c. fresh or frozen cut
   green beans
1 c. carrots, peeled and sliced
1/2 c. fresh parsley, chopped
8-oz. pkg. fine egg noodles,
   uncooked
1/4 c. butter, sliced
1/4 c. all-purpose flour

Place turkey carcass in a large soup pot, breaking to fit if necessary. Add water, celery and celery leaves, onion, bouillon, salt, pepper and bay leaf. Bring to a boil over high heat; reduce heat to medium-low. Cover and simmer for one hour, stirring occasionally. Remove carcass to a platter; let cool. To reserved broth in soup pot, add vegetables and parsley. Return to a boil; reduce heat to medium and simmer for 10 minutes. Meanwhile, cut or scrape meat from carcass; add meat to soup pot. Add more water if needed. Bring to a boil; stir in noodles and cook, uncovered, for 10 minutes. Melt butter in a small frying pan, stir in flour. Cook over low heat, stirring constantly, until flour browns lightly. Stir into boiling soup. When the soup returns to a boil, reduce heat and simmer for 5 minutes. Discard bay leaf. Serve hot in large bowls. Makes 10 to 12 servings.

Discard bay leaves easily before serving soup. Tuck them into a metal tea ball that can hang on the side of the pot. Simple to remove when done!

Warm & Cozy
Soups & Breads

Easy Yeast Rolls

Andrea Hickerson
Trenton, TN

So quick & easy! Perfect for dinnertime or with a bowl of soup.

1 c. plus 2 T. warm water, about
   110 to 115 degrees
1/3 c. oil
2 T. active dry yeast

1/4 c. sugar
1/2 t. salt
1 egg, beaten
3-1/2 c. bread flour

Combine warm water, oil, yeast and sugar in the bowl of a stand mixer
with a dough hook. Stir to combine; allow to rest for 15 minutes. With
mixer on medium speed, add salt, egg and flour. Knead with dough
hook for about 2 to 3 minutes, until flour is thoroughly mixed in and
dough is soft and smooth. Divide dough into 12 balls; place on a
greased baking sheet. Allow to rest for 10 minutes. Bake at 375 degrees
for 7 minutes, or until golden. Makes one dozen.

Cream Cheese Poppy Seed Rolls

Teri Austin
Yukon, OK

I've served these rolls at a ladies' luncheon.
They're very good alongside hot soup.

1/4 c. butter, softened
2 c. self-rising flour
1 c. whole milk

8-oz. pkg. cream cheese,
   room temperature
1-1/2 t. poppy seed

Generously coat muffin cups with softened butter; set aside. In a bowl,
mix flour, milk, cream cheese and poppy seed until well blended. Spoon
batter into muffin cups, filling 3/4 full. Bake at 350 degrees until golden,
25 to 30 minutes for regular muffins. Makes one dozen.

As autumn evenings turn dark,
light a candle or two at the family
dinner table. It'll make an ordinary
meal seem special!

Fall Cooking
with *Family & Friends*

Tasty Sausage, Bean & Spinach Soup

Rosemary Lightbown
Wakefield, RI

Chock-full of of hearty ingredients, this soup is a meal in itself, perfect for a cold day. I sometimes add 1/3 cup ditalini pasta as it's simmering. Serve with crusty bread.

1 lb. Italian pork sausage links, sliced 1/2-inch thick
1/4 c. water
1 T. oil
1/2 c. onion, chopped
2 to 3 cloves garlic, minced
32-oz. container chicken broth
14-1/2 oz. can diced tomatoes
2 15-1/2 oz. cans cannellini beans, drained and rinsed
4 c. fresh spinach or kale, chopped
1 t. dried oregano
1 t. dried parsley
1 t. dried basil
pepper to taste

Combine sausage and water in a large pot over medium-high heat. Bring to a boil; cover and cook for 10 minutes. Uncover; cook for another 5 minutes, or until sausage is browned. Remove sausage to a plate; drain skillet. Add oil to skillet and heat over medium heat. Add onion and garlic; cook for 5 minutes, or until tender. Stir in chicken broth, tomatoes with juice and beans; bring to a boil. Reduce heat to low and simmer for 15 minutes. Stir in sausage, spinach or kale and herbs. Simmer for 5 minutes, or until spinach or kale is wilted. Season with pepper. Makes 8 servings.

October is crisp days and cool nights, a time to curl up around the dancing flames and sink into a good book.

-John Sinor

Warm & Cozy
Soups & Breads

Slow-Cooker French Onion Soup

Marsha Kent
Chapin, SC

I made this delicious soup one day in September, 2020, when we had a gloomy, rainy day here in South Carolina due to Hurricane Sally! If you like, broil the bowls of soup until the cheese is melted and golden. I don't find this step necessary.

1/4 c. butter
3 c. onions, sliced
2 T. all-purpose flour
1 T. sugar
1 t. salt
4 c. beef broth
1/4 c. white wine or beef broth

1 t. Worcestershire sauce
1/2 t. dried thyme
1 t. garlic, minced
1 bay leaf
6 slices French bread
1 c. shredded Gruyère cheese

Melt butter in a skillet over medium heat. Add onions; sprinkle with flour, sugar and salt. Cook, stirring often, until onions are dark golden. Spoon onion mixture into a 4-quart slow cooker; add remaining ingredients except bread and cheese. Cover and cook on high setting for 4 hours. Discard bay leaf. To serve, place bread slices in 6 bowls; ladle hot soup over bread. Sprinkle cheese on top. Makes 6 servings.

Tin cans with colorful, vintage-style labels make the best country-style vases. Tuck small bouquets of mums into several cans and line them up along a windowsill or group them on a table.

Bean Soup Fit For Company

Lisanne Miller
Wells, ME

I love to have this hearty meatless soup simmering in my slow cooker when friends come over to watch football or pick apples. Serve with cornbread or tortilla chips. Heat it up again the next day for great flavor. Apple pie is a great dessert with this soup!

15-1/2 oz. can hot ranch-style
    chili beans
15-1/2 oz. can red kidney beans
15-1/2 oz. can white kidney
    beans
15-1/2 oz. can black beans
15-1/2 oz. can pinto beans
2 32-oz. cans petite diced
    tomatoes
2 t. garlic, minced

3 to 4 carrots, peeled and
    chopped
1 stalk celery, chopped
2 T. fresh parsley, chopped
1 env. mild taco seasoning mix
1/2 t. pepper
Optional: sour cream, shredded
    cheese, sliced jalapeño
    peppers

Combine canned beans and tomatoes in a 6-quart slow cooker; do not drain any cans. Add garlic, carrots, celery, parsley, taco seasoning and pepper; mix well. Cover and cook on high setting for 6 hours, or on low setting for 8 hours or overnight. At serving time, add toppings as desired. Serves 6.

Watch tag sales for a big red speckled enamelware stockpot...
it's just the right size for cooking up a family-size batch of soup.
The bright color adds a homey touch to any soup supper!

Cheeseburger Chowder

Joanne Mauseth
Clear Lake, SD

My mom, my three sisters and my daughter would all get together after Thanksgiving to do our holiday baking. It was always so much more fun when we baked together! I always made this soup and kept it warm in the slow cooker while we were working, then as each of us had time, we would eat our lunch. It is filled with great flavor. The recipe is easily doubled to make more servings.

1 lb. ground beef
1-1/2 c. water
2 to 3 cubes beef bouillon
1/2 t. salt
2 potatoes, peeled and diced
1/2 c. celery, diced

1/2 onion, diced
1/2 green pepper, diced
3 T. all-purpose flour
2-1/2 c. milk, divided
1 c. shredded Cheddar cheese

Brown beef in a soup kettle over medium heat; drain. Add water, bouillon, salt and vegetables. Cover and cook for 15 to 20 minutes, stirring occasionally, until vegetables are tender. Blend flour into 1/2 cup milk; add to kettle along with remaining milk. Cook and stir until thickened. Add cheese; stir until melted. Makes 4 servings.

Turn bowls of soup into spiderweb soup! Spoon sour cream into a plastic zipping bag. Snip off one corner and pipe the sour cream in circles on the soup. To create a web effect, pull a toothpick across the circles, starting in the center.

Fall Cooking
with *Family & Friends*

Company Taco Soup

Kharla Sherman
Benham, KY

Any time I need to feed company quickly, this is my go-to recipe. This warm and filling soup goes a long way and is always a crowd-pleaser. It's perfect for a game night, or for watching ballgames together. Just add tortilla chips and toppings to complete the dish.

2 lbs. lean ground beef
2 15-1/2 oz. cans mild chili
  beans
2 15-1/2 oz. cans tomato sauce
14-1/2 oz. can diced tomatoes
  with mild green chiles
15-1/2 oz. can black beans,
  drained
14-3/4 oz. can corn, drained
2 c. water

1-1/4 oz. pkg. taco seasoning
  mix
1-oz. pkg. ranch dip mix
1 t. chili powder
1/2 c. instant rice, uncooked
salt and pepper to taste
Garnish: shredded Cheddar
  cheese, sour cream
tortilla chips

Brown and crumble beef in a large soup pot over medium heat; drain. Add undrained chili beans, tomato sauce, undrained tomatoes, black beans, corn, water, seasoning mixes and chili powder. Stir well. Bring to a boil; reduce heat to medium. Simmer for 20 to 30 minutes, stirring occasionally. Add extra water to desired consistency, if necessary. About 10 minutes before soup has finished simmering, stir in rice; season with salt and pepper. To serve, top with shredded cheese and sour cream; serve with tortilla chips on the side. Serves 10.

Share the warmth! With winter on the way, autumn is
a perfect time to pull outgrown coats, hats and mittens
out of closets and donate them to a local charity.

Warm & Cozy
Soups & Breads

Mexicali Pepper Muffins

Vickie
Gooseberry Patch

With the zesty kick of peppers, these spicy snacks are sure to tide you over until dinnertime! They're great with soup too.

1/4 c. green pepper,
  finely chopped
1/4 c. yellow pepper,
  finely chopped
1/4 c. red pepper, finely chopped
1/4 c. fresh or frozen corn
1/4 c. butter
1 c. yellow cornmeal

1 c. all-purpose flour
2 T. sugar
1 T. baking powder
1/2 t. salt
1/2 t. chili powder
1/2 t. dried basil
2 eggs, beaten
1 c. milk

In a skillet over medium heat, sauté peppers and corn in butter for 3 to 4 minutes. Meanwhile, in a large bowl, stir together cornmeal, flour, sugar, baking powder, salt and seasonings. In another bowl, beat together eggs and milk. Add egg mixture and pepper mixture to flour mixture; stir until moistened. Pour batter into greased muffin cups, filling 2/3 full. Bake at 400 degrees for 15 to 20 minutes, until golden. Makes one dozen.

A baker's secret! Grease muffin cups on the bottoms and just halfway up the sides. Muffins will bake up nicely puffed on top.

Fall Cooking
with *Family & Friends*

French Market Soup

Debby Marcum
Gosport, IN

This soup is wonderful to enjoy while watching a Sunday night football game! I love to simmer mine all afternoon for the flavors to really develop. Be sure to serve it with a dollop of sour cream and some warm crusty bread. It's even better the next day!

20-oz. pkg. 15-bean soup mix,
   rinsed and sorted
1 lb. boneless, skinless chicken
   breasts, chopped
1 lb. smoked pork sausage, sliced
1 lb. cooked ham, diced
14-1/2 oz. can diced tomatoes

8 c. water
1 onion, finely chopped
1 clove garlic, minced
1/4 t. dried oregano
1/4 t. cinnamon
1/2 t. salt
Garnish: sour cream

In a large soup pot, combine all ingredients except garnish, adding seasoning packet from beans. (There's no need to soak beans or brown meats.) Bring to a boil over high heat; reduce heat to medium-low. Simmer for 2-1/2 to 3 hours, stirring occasionally, until beans are soft. Garnish servings with a dollop of sour cream. Makes 8 to 10 servings.

Do you have lots of leftover holiday turkey? It freezes well for up to 3 months. Cut turkey into bite-size pieces, place in plastic freezer bags and pop in the freezer...ready to stir into hearty soups and casseroles whenever you are.

Warm & Cozy
Soups & Breads

Cheesy Chicken Noodle Soup
Andrea Heyart
Savannah, TX

When a dish like this soup calls to me, I like to buy a rotisserie chicken from the supermarket, pick the meat off the bones and keep the chicken on hand for busy nights. It makes an easy dish even more simple!

2 T. butter
1/2 white onion, diced
32-oz. container chicken broth
32-oz. container vegetable broth
16-oz. pkg. pasteurized process
   cheese, cubed

3-lb. deli rotisserie chicken,
   diced or shredded
12-oz. pkg. egg noodles,
   uncooked

Melt butter in a large stockpot over medium heat. Add onion; cook over medium heat until translucent and tender. Add broths; bring to a gentle boil. Add cheese and cook, stirring constantly, until melted. Stir in chicken and noodles; cook for another 10 minutes, until noodles are cooked through. Makes 6 to 8 servings.

Bacon-Sour Cream Roll-Ups
Irene Robinson
Cincinnati, OH

My grandchildren love these little morsels alongside a bowl of cream of tomato soup. These are also great as appetizers.

1/2 lb. bacon, crisply cooked
   and crumbled
1/2 c. sour cream

1/8 t. garlic powder
8-oz. tube refrigerated
   crescent rolls

Combine crumbled bacon, sour cream and garlic powder in a bowl; mix well. Cover and chill for one to 2 hours. Separate crescent rolls into 4 rectangles; spread mixture over rectangles. Roll up, starting with one long side. Slice each roll into 6 pieces. Place cut-side down on an ungreased baking sheet. Bake at 375 degrees for 11 to 13 minutes, until golden. Serve warm. Makes 2 dozen.

Fall Cooking
with *Family & Friends*

Harvest Salmon Chowder
Jane Martin
Havre de Grace, MD

This is my sister's recipe (thanks, Lin!) and we've both been making it for years. Even my vegetable-challenged husband loves this comforting soup on a chilly fall day.

3 T. butter
1/2 c. onion, chopped
1/2 c. celery, chopped
1/4 c. green pepper, chopped
1 clove garlic, minced
1 c. potatoes, peeled and diced
1 c. carrots, peeled and diced

2 c. chicken broth
1-1/2 t. salt
3/4 t. pepper
1 t. dried dill weed
7-3/4 oz. can salmon, flaked
12-oz. can evaporated milk
8-1/4 oz. can cream-style corn

Melt butter in a large saucepan over medium heat. Sauté onion, celery and green pepper until tender. Add garlic; cook for one more minute. Add potatoes, carrots, chicken broth and seasonings. Cover and simmer for 20 minutes, stirring occasionally. Add flaked salmon with liquid, evaporated milk and corn. Heat through over low heat, stirring constantly. Serves 4 to 6.

Serve tasty soft pretzels with soup. Twist strips of refrigerated bread stick dough into pretzel shapes and place on an ungreased baking sheet. Brush with beaten egg white, sprinkle with coarse salt and bake as directed.

Warm & Cozy
Soups & Breads

New England Clam Chowder

Barbara Klein
Newburgh, IN

I love this slow-cooker recipe for clam chowder.
It's absolutely delicious and very easy to make.

1 to 2 6-1/2 oz. cans
    chopped clams
2 10-3/4 oz. cans New England
    clam chowder
2 10-3/4 oz. cans cream of
    potato soup

10-3/4 oz. can cream of
    celery soup
12-oz. can evaporated milk
1/2 c. butter, sliced
1-1/4 c. water
dried parsley to taste

Combine undrained clams and remaining ingredients in a 4-quart slow cooker; stir well. Cover and cook on low setting for 2 to 2-1/2 hours, stirring occasionally. May also simply heat through in a saucepan on the stovetop; do not allow to boil. Serves 6 to 8.

Easy Crab Bisque

Tonya Sheppard
Galveston, TX

Ready in 20 minutes! Serve in cups for a tasty warmer-upper.

10-3/4 oz. can cream of
    mushroom soup
10-3/4 oz. can cream of
    asparagus soup
2-3/4 c. milk

1 c. half-and-half
6-1/2 oz. can crabmeat, drained
    and flaked
3 T. dry sherry or milk
Garnish: paprika

In a large saucepan over medium heat, whisk together soups, milk and half-and-half. Bring just to a boil, stirring often. Stir in crabmeat and sherry or milk; heat through. Garnish with a sprinkle of paprika. Makes 6 to 8 servings.

Keep a thermos of soup toasty warm. Fill the thermos with hot water and let stand for 10 minutes. Pour out the water, add hot soup and the lid...ready for tailgating!

Fall Cooking
with Family & Friends

Mom's Vegetable Soup

Joyce Keeling
Springfield, MO

This is one of my favorite soups to enjoy on chilly, rainy nights. Although it is called Vegetable Soup, Mom always added browned ground beef to it. She used her own home-canned tomatoes. We'd always have plenty of buttered, crusty homemade bread to dip in it. So, so good!

1 lb. ground beef
2 potatoes, peeled and diced
15-oz. can mixed vegetables,
   drained
1/3 c. long-cooking rice,
   uncooked

salt and pepper to taste
2 c. hot water
14-1/2 oz. can stewed tomatoes
46-oz. bottle cocktail vegetable
   juice
Optional: 1 t. sugar

Brown beef in a Dutch oven over medium heat; drain. Add potatoes, mixed vegetables, rice, salt and pepper. Add enough hot water to cover, adding more water if needed as soup cooks down. Reduce heat to medium-low; simmer for 20 minutes, or until potatoes are tender. Stir in undrained tomatoes and vegetable juice. Stir in sugar if tomatoes are too tart. Simmer until heated through. Makes 4 servings.

Old quilts, buffalo check blankets and blanket-stitched
throws make the best spreads for an outdoor
autumn picnic or tailgating party!

Maple-Cream Cheese Muffins

*Eleanor Dionne
Beverly, MA*

One of my favorites through the years. I like the cream cheese filling, and the whole-wheat flour makes it a little different.

1/4 c. cream cheese, softened	1/2 t. salt
2 T. pure maple syrup	1-1/4 c. buttermilk
1-1/2 c. all-purpose flour	1/4 c. canola oil
1/2 c. whole-wheat flour	2 egg whites, beaten
2 t. baking powder	1/4 c. sugar
1/2 t. baking soda	

In a small bowl, beat together cream cheese and syrup; set aside. In a large bowl, sift together flours, baking powder, baking soda and salt; set aside. In another bowl, whisk together buttermilk, oil, egg whites and sugar; add to flour mixture and stir all together. Spoon batter into greased muffin cups, filling 1/4 full. Drop a teaspoonful of cream cheese mixture into the center of each muffin; add remaining batter to fill cups 2/3 full. Bake at 375 degrees for 20 to 25 minutes. Makes 10 muffins.

Top a salad with grilled apple slices...yummy! Heat a tablespoon each of olive oil and maple syrup in a grill pan. Add thin slices of tart apple. Cook for 6 to 8 minutes, turning once, until crisp and deeply golden. Serve warm.

Fall Cooking
with *Family & Friends*

Cindy's White Chili

Cindy Ketron
Kingsport, TN

Thirty years ago, I tasted a delicious white chili at a restaurant. I began experimenting until I had virtually replicated the restaurant chili. It's easy and tasty...I've won a local award for it! Because I use an already-cooked chicken and a prepared mix, this recipe can easily be tossed together in 10 minutes or less. My family loves it! Sometimes I'll add sliced mushrooms.

4 15-1/2 oz. cans Great
    Northern, navy, cannellini
    and/or garbanzo beans
3 10-3/4 oz. cans bean with
    bacon soup
1-1/4 oz. pkg. white chicken
    chili seasoning mix

2 to 3 c. water
3-lb. deli rotisserie chicken,
    shredded or chopped
2 c. shredded Cheddar cheese
Garnish: sour cream, crushed
    corn chips

Add undrained beans to a 5-quart slow cooker. Stir in bean soup, chili mix, 2 cups water, chicken and cheese. Cover and cook on low setting for 3 hours. Add remaining water, if needed. Garnish with sour cream and corn ships. Serves 8 to 12.

Easy Cheesy Cornbread

Nancy Hanson
Murrieta, CA

This is a delicious, moist recipe that's always asked for at every dinner I take it to.

1/2 c. cream cheese, softened
3/4 c. milk
8-1/2 oz. pkg. corn muffin mix
3 eggs, beaten

15-1/4 oz. can corn, drained
14-3/4 oz. can cream-style corn
1 c. shredded Cheddar cheese

In a large bowl, blend cream cheese and milk until smooth. Stir in dry muffin mix and remaining ingredients until blended. Pour batter into a 13"x9" baking pan sprayed with non-stick vegetable spray. Bake at 375 degrees for 34 to 36 minutes, until golden. Cut into squares. Serves 8 to 12.

Potluck
Sides &
Salads

Fall Cooking
with *Family & Friends*

Yam, Apple & Pineapple Casserole

Janis Parr
Ontario Canada

This is a really tasty dish that's easy to prepare and a nice change from other sides. I've made it using coarsely chopped, cooked butternut squash instead of the yams...it's delicious this way too.

32-oz. can cut yams, drained
5 Northern Spy or McIntosh
   apples, peeled, cored and
   sliced
20-oz. can pineapple chunks,
   drained and 1/2 cup liquid
   reserved

1 c. brown sugar, packed
1/2 c. sugar
5 T. butter, sliced
1/2 t. salt

In a buttered 3-quart casserole dish, layer yams, apple slices and pineapple chunks; set aside. In a small saucepan over low heat, combine sugars, butter, salt and reserved pineapple juice. Stir well; cook until sugars are dissolved. Pour evenly over yam mixture. Bake, uncovered, at 350 degrees for 50 minutes, or until bubbly and glazed. Serve hot. Makes 6 to 8 servings.

Whimsical napkin rings...tie ears of red-kerneled strawberry popcorn with a raffia bow and lay on folded napkins.

Bacon & Swiss Tossed Salad

Michele Shenk
Manheim, PA

We enjoy this salad any time of the year! It's very tasty and easy to prepare, and the ingredients are always available.

1/2 c. mayonnaise
1 T. sugar
1/4 t. salt
1/4 t. pepper
6 c. mixed salad greens, divided
3/4 c. red onion, sliced

10-oz. pkg. frozen peas, thawed
8-oz. pkg. Swiss cheese, cut into
    thin strips
1/2 to 1 lb. bacon, crisply cooked
    and crumbled

In a small bowl, mix mayonnaise, sugar, salt and pepper; set aside. In a large bowl, layer 1/3 of salad greens, 1/3 of mayonnaise mixture and all of onion, peas and cheese. Repeat layering of greens and mayonnaise mixture twice. Cover and refrigerate for at least 2 hours. Just before serving, add bacon and toss. Serves 6 to 8.

For fall fun, pack a picnic lunch, grab your sweaters and take
the family on a trip to an apple orchard. Pick your own apples,
go on a wagon ride and sample fresh-pressed cider...
what a sweet way to make memories together!

Fall Cooking
with Family & Friends

Prize Potato Casserole

Joyce Roebuck
Jacksonville, TX

This dish won "First Place" in the side dish category
in a local cooking contest, several years ago.

10 green onions, chopped
1/2 c. butter
2 10-3/4 oz. cans cream of
　mushroom soup
2 4-oz. cans sliced mushrooms

1 c. whipping cream
1/2 t. salt
1/2 t. pepper
8 to 12 potatoes, peeled
　and sliced

In a skillet over medium heat, sauté onions in butter. Add mushroom soup and mushrooms; mix well and remove from heat. Stir in cream, salt and pepper. In a buttered 13"x9" baking pan, layer 1/3 each of sliced potatoes and warm sauce; repeat layering twice. Cover and bake at 350 degrees for 1-1/2 hours; uncover during the last 15 minutes. Makes 10 to 12 servings.

Corn Niblets in Butter Sauce

Barb Rudyk
Alberta, Canada

Make your own scrumptious corn in butter sauce. Perfect for
a holiday meal! This recipe makes a lot, but it's easy to halve.

2 16-oz. pkgs. frozen corn
2 t. salt
1/2 c. butter, sliced

1 t. sugar
1 c. cold water
1-1/2 t. cornstarch

In a large saucepan, combine all ingredients except water and cornstarch. Cook and stir over medium heat until butter is melted. Combine water and cornstarch in a cup. Stir until cornstarch is dissolved; slowly add to mixture in saucepan, stirring constantly. Reduce heat to medium-low; cook and stir until sauce thickens. Simmer, stirring occasionally, until corn is tender, about 10 minutes. Serves 10 to 12.

Sides & Salads

Cauliflower au Gratin

Cindy Cluchie
Cavalier, ND

My daughter hated cauliflower growing up. Now this is one of her favorites! It's a good side dish with beef, chicken or pork.

1 head cauliflower, cut into
   bite-size flowerets
1/2 c. cream cheese, softened
1/4 c. milk
1/2 c. sour cream

1-1/2 c. shredded sharp Cheddar
   cheese
10 buttery club crackers, crushed
3 T. grated Parmesan cheese

In a large saucepan, cover cauliflower with water. Bring to a boil over high heat; reduce heat to medium and cook until fork-tender. Drain well and set aside. In a bowl, combine cream cheese, milk, sour cream and Cheddar cheese. Mix well; add to cauliflower and toss to coat. Transfer to a greased 2-quart casserole dish. Combine cracker crumbs and Parmesan cheese; sprinkle on top. Bake, uncovered, at 350 degrees for 25 minutes, or until bubbly and golden. Makes 6 to 8 servings.

A hollowed-out pumpkin makes a fun flower vase...try other hard winter squashes too! Cut an opening at the top of the squash and slip in a small plastic cup or a floral tube. Fill with flowers and add water to keep them fresh.

Fall Cooking
with *Family & Friends*

Crispy Bacon & Pear Salad

Lynda Hart
Bluffdale, UT

This salad is great anytime, but especially in the fall.

1/2 c. walnut halves
2 Red Bartlett pears, cored and
   sliced lengthwise
1 T. lemon juice

6 slices bacon, crisply cooked
   and crumbled
1 c. watercress leaves, tough
   stalks removed

Toast walnuts in a dry skillet over medium heat for 2 to 3 minutes; set aside to cool. In a salad bowl, toss pear slices with lemon juice. Add walnuts, crumbled bacon and watercress; toss to mix. Pour Dressing over salad and toss to combine. Chill and serve. Serves 4.

Dressing:

3 T. olive oil
2 T. lemon juice
1/2 t. honey

1/2 t. salt
1/2 t. pepper
Optional: 1/4 t. cinnamon

Whisk together oil, lemon juice and honey. Season with salt, pepper and cinnamon, if desired.

Not what we say about our blessings, but how we use them,
is the true measure of our thanksgiving.
–W.T. Purkiser

Tiffany's Tasty Succotash

Tiffany Jones
Batesville, AR

I saw this dish at an amusement park my family likes to visit and it always looked scrumptious. So I came up with my own version and oh my...it's so delicious. A definite keeper!

1/2 c. onion, chopped
1/2 c. green pepper, chopped
1/2 c. butter
10-oz. can diced tomatoes with
    green chiles

10-oz. pkg. frozen corn
10-oz. pkg. frozen lima beans
10-oz. pkg. frozen sliced okra

In a large saucepan over medium heat, sauté onion and pepper in butter until tender. Add tomatoes with juice and remaining ingredients. Cook over medium heat until tender, about 15 minutes, stirring occasionally. Makes 6 to 8 servings.

If the weather report calls for frost and there are still green tomatoes in the garden, don't fret! Pick them, wrap individually in newspaper and place in a brown paper bag. They'll be ripe and red in a week or so.

Fall Cooking
with Family & Friends

Super Spinach Casserole

Shirley Howie
Foxboro, MA

*This is a great side dish that goes well with just about anything!
I like to serve it with baked chicken breasts and a tossed
salad, for a really healthy, tasty meal.*

2 t. butter
1/4 c. onion, chopped
2 eggs, beaten
1/2 c. milk

1/3 c. grated Parmesan cheese
1 c. cooked white rice
10-oz. pkg. frozen chopped
   spinach, thawed and drained

Melt butter in a skillet over medium heat. Add onion; cook for 5 minutes,
or until soft. In a bowl, combine eggs, milk and Parmesan cheese; mix
well. Add onion mixture, rice and spinach; mix well and transfer to a
greased 1-1/2 quart casserole dish. Bake, uncovered, at 350 degrees
for 35 minutes, or until heated through. Serves 6.

Scalloped Brussels Sprouts

Teresa Verell
Roanoke, VA

*This recipe is a family favorite...it's always requested
for our Thanksgiving dinner.*

10-3/4 oz. can cream of
   mushroom soup
1/2 c. fat-free half-and-half
1/8 t. pepper

16-oz. pkg. frozen Brussels
   sprouts, thawed
8 slices bacon, crisply cooked
   and crumbled

In a large skillet, combine soup, half-and-half and pepper. Cook over
medium heat for 5 minutes, stirring occasionally. Stir in Brussels
sprouts; simmer over low heat for 10 minutes, or until tender. Top
with crumbled bacon and serve. Makes 4 servings.

Make a quick cheese sauce for veggies. Combine one cup evaporated
milk and 1/2 cup shredded cheese in a saucepan...cook and
stir over low heat until smooth.

Potluck
Sides & Salads

Almond Green Beans with Mushrooms

Kathy Courington
Canton, GA

My husband likes green beans, and he loves these with the crunch of almonds. Easy for everyday, yet good enough for company!

1/2 c. shallots or onion, chopped
1-1/2 c. sliced mushrooms
1/4 c. slivered almonds, divided
10-3/4 oz. can cream of
  mushroom soup

2 14-1/2 oz. cans cut green
  beans, drained
1/4 t. pepper

Spray a large skillet with non-stick vegetable spray. Add shallots or onion; sauté over medium heat for 5 minutes, or until tender. Add mushrooms and half of almonds; stir. Cook for 2 to 3 minutes. Stir in mushroom soup, green beans and pepper. Reduce heat to medium-low and simmer for 5 minutes, stirring occasionally, or until mixture is heated through. Top with remaining almonds and serve. Serves 4.

KK's Green Bean Casserole

Kay Daugherty
Collinsville, MS

I have a sweet niece who expects this casserole every Thanksgiving on our family table. I enjoy making it for this special reason. It's a special addition to the dinner table anytime.

3 14-1/2 oz. cans French-style
  green beans, drained
10-3/4 oz. can cream of
  mushroom soup
8-oz. container sour cream

1 c. shredded sharp Cheddar
  cheese
6-oz. can French fried onions,
  divided

In a large bowl, mix together green beans, mushroom soup, sour cream, cheese and half the onions. Spread mixture evenly in a greased 2-quart casserole dish. Bake, uncovered, at 350 degrees for 40 minutes. Top with remaining onions; bake for an additional 15 minutes, or until bubbly and golden. Serves 8.

Fall Cooking
with *Family & Friends*

Fresh Tomato Salad

Stephanie Nilsen
Fremont, NE

This salad is so easy to make. It's best with fresh, home-grown tomatoes, but store-bought also makes a good salad! The roma tomatoes can be replaced with a pint of cherry tomatoes, halved.

4 roma tomatoes, cubed
1/2 yellow onion, thinly sliced
3 T. olive oil
1/4 t. rice wine vinegar

1 clove garlic, minced
1 t. dried oregano
1/2 to 1 t. salt, to taste

Combine tomatoes and onion in a bowl; set aside. Mix remaining ingredients in a cup and pour over tomato mixture; mix gently. Cover and chill until serving time. For best flavor, don't refrigerate overnight, as the tomatoes tend to get mushy. Makes 4 servings.

Hosting the next book club meeting with friends? Serve a salad luncheon for a change of pace...try a pasta salad, a chicken or tuna salad and a tossed salad. A loaf of quick bread and and a simple dessert complete a meal that's sure to be enjoyed.

Creamy Coleslaw with Poppy Seed

JoAnn
Gooseberry Patch

My family loves restaurant-style coleslaw. They agree that this one is a keeper! Great for casual dinners and potlucks.

16-oz. pkg. shredded
   coleslaw mix
2 T. onion, diced
2/3 c. mayonnaise-style salad
   dressing

3 T. oil
1/2 c. sugar
1 T. white vinegar
1/2 t. poppy seed
1/4 t. salt

Combine coleslaw mix and onion in a large bowl; set aside. In another bowl, whisk together remaining ingredients; blend thoroughly. Spoon dressing mixture over coleslaw and toss to coat. Cover and chill at least 2 hours before serving. Serves 8.

Adding raw onions to a salad? Slice or chop ahead of time, place in a glass jar and cover with some of the salad dressing you'll use. At serving time, drain and toss with the salad. Onions will stay crisp and lose some of the strong taste.

Roasted Fall Vegetables

Doreen Knapp
Stanfordville, NY

*I love roasted vegetables! I could eat them as a meal or on some
flatbread. They always make a great add-in to chili and soup. I even
love leftover roasted vegetables with eggs the next morning.*

1 lb. redskin potatoes, cubed
2 c. butternut squash, peeled and
   cut into 1-inch cubes
2 to 3 carrots, peeled and cut into
   1/2-inch rounds
2 to 3 parsnips, peeled and cut
   into 1/2-inch rounds
3 T. olive oil
1 T. fresh rosemary, snipped,
   or 1 t. dried rosemary
2 cloves fresh garlic, minced
1/2 t. kosher salt
1/4 t. cracked pepper
2 to 3 c. fresh kale, chopped
1 red onion, halved and
   separated into crescents

In a large bowl, combine all ingredients except kale and onion; toss to
coat with oil. Spread evenly on 2 parchment paper-lined large rimmed
baking sheets. Set on separate oven racks; bake at 400 degrees for
15 minutes. Divide kale and onion between baking sheets; stir well.
Return to oven, rotating trays; bake for another 15 minutes, or until
vegetables are easily pierced with a knife tip. Makes 4 to 6 servings.

Set a plump pillar candle in an old-fashioned punched tin
lantern, and enjoy a soft glow on a dark autumn night.

Easy Vegetable Rice Pilaf

Shirley Howie
Foxboro, MA

This healthy, easy-to-make side dish goes well with just about anything, and the turmeric gives it a lovely color! You can substitute any frozen veggie you like for the peas and carrots. I sometimes use corn and green beans for variety.

1 T. olive oil
3 T. onion, diced
1 c. long-cooking white rice, uncooked
1/2 t. garlic salt

1/2 t. dried basil
1/2 t. turmeric
2 c. chicken broth
1 c. frozen peas & carrots

In a large saucepan, heat oil over medium heat. Add onion and cook for about 3 minutes, until translucent. Add rice; cook and stir until rice is lightly toasted. Add seasonings to skillet and stir until evenly combined. Stir in chicken broth and bring to a boil. Reduce heat to a medium-low, cover and cook for 10 minutes. Stir in frozen peas and carrots; cover and cook for an additional 10 minutes. Fluff rice with a fork and serve. Serves 6.

Keep little ones busy and happy while the grown-ups get dinner ready. Set out paper plates to decorate with colored paper, feathers, pom-poms, crayons and washable glue. At dinnertime, they'll be proud to display their creations!

Fall Cooking
with *Family & Friends*

Nana's Thanksgiving Stuffing

Rachel Evans
Beavercreek, OH

My grandmother made several batches of her stuffing each year, because it was everyone's favorite! She has been gone now for more than 20 years, but this recipe helps us feel like she is still around for the holidays. We always share stories about her around the dinner table, while eating our favorite Nana's Thanksgiving Stuffing.

12-oz. pkg. seasoned stuffing
14-1/2 oz. can chicken broth
2 eggs, beaten
2/3 c. butter, melted

4 to 5 stalks celery, diced
3 T. dried, chopped onions
1/2 t. poultry seasoning
1/4 t. pepper

Mix all ingredients together in a bowl; stir until evenly coated. Spoon mixture into a greased 13"x9" baking pan. Bake, uncovered, at 350 degrees for 30 minutes, or until heated through. Makes 8 to 10 servings.

If it's Thanksgiving now, Christmas isn't far away. Why not double any must-have casseroles or side dishes and freeze half for Christmas dinner...you'll be so glad you did!

Grandy's Sweet Potato Casserole

Carolyn Tellers
Erie, PA

Our family used to love when Grandy made this for Thanksgiving dinner. I've made it for family gatherings too. It's delicious!

3 c. mashed sweet potatoes
5 T. plus 1/4 c. melted butter, divided
3 eggs, beaten
1/4 to 1/2 c. sugar
1/2 t. nutmeg
1/2 t. cinnamon
1 c. brown sugar, packed
1/2 c. all-purpose flour
1 c. chopped walnuts

In a bowl, combine mashed sweet potatoes, 5 tablespoons melted butter, eggs, sugar and spices. Mix well and spread in a greased 13"x9" baking pan. Combine remaining butter, brown sugar, flour and walnuts; spread over sweet potatoes. Bake, uncovered, at 350 degrees for 30 to 40 minutes, until bubbly and golden. Serves 8.

Green Bean Wraps

Sherrye Walker
Trezevant, TN

For the past 20 years, I've made this recipe every Thanksgiving for our luncheon at work. It is always requested and always enjoyed. I prefer thinner sliced bacon, it just seems to work better.

1 lb. thin-sliced bacon, slices cut into halves or thirds
3 to 4 14-1/2 oz. cans whole green beans, drained
1/2 c. butter
1 c. brown sugar, packed
1 t. soy sauce
1/2 t. garlic powder

Wrap each piece of bacon around 5 to 6 beans. Arrange in a lightly greased 13"x9" baking pan and set aside. Melt butter in a saucepan over medium-low heat; add remaining ingredients. Cook and stir until brown sugar is dissolved; spoon over beans in pan. Bake, uncovered, at 375 degrees for 30 to 45 minutes, until hot and bacon is lightly golden. Serves 6 to 8.

Fall Cooking
with *Family & Friends*

Spicy Parmesan Pasta Salad

Jimmy Cox
Westfield, IN

I made this recipe for my wife, Megan, in our first year of marriage, just experimenting. She loves spicy food, so her favorite part of the recipe is the crushed red pepper flakes. It's very good...give it a try!

12-oz. pkg. tri-color rotini
　pasta, uncooked
1 red pepper, diced
1 orange pepper, diced
3-1/2 oz. pkg. pepperoni slices,
　quartered

16-oz. bottle zesty Italian salad
　dressing, divided
1/2 c. red pepper flakes, or to
　taste
1 c. grated Parmesan cheese

Cook pasta according to package directions. Drain; rinse in cold water and drain again. Transfer pasta to a large bowl. Add peppers, pepperoni and 3/4 of salad dressing to pasta and mix. Add desired amount of red pepper flakes and mix. Add Parmesan cheese and mix. Cover and refrigerate for 4 or more hours. At serving time, add remaining salad dressing; toss to mix well. Serves 15 to 20.

For a simple and splendid decoration, scatter pressed autumn leaves
on a crisp white tablecloth. Layer leaves between paper towels,
then between sections of newspaper. Top with a heavy book...
leaves will be ready in a week or so. If time is short,
substitute silk leaves from the craft store.

Favorite Artichoke Heart Salad

Paula Marchesi
Auburn, PA

This delicious salad is so quick & easy to make. Whenever I'm in a pinch because unexpected guests have arrived, it's my go-to salad. It only uses five ingredients, and I always have them on hand.

2 14-oz. cans artichoke hearts, drained and quartered
2 2-1/4 oz. cans sliced black olives, drained
2/3 c. green or red pepper, chopped
2/3 c. green onions, thinly sliced
1-1/2 c. Italian salad dressing

In a large bowl, combine artichokes, olives, pepper and onions. Add salad dressing; toss to coat. Cover and refrigerate for at least 30 to 40 minutes. Serve with a slotted spoon. Serves 6 to 8.

Winter is coming! Fill the pantry with canned vegetables, creamy soups, rice mixes, boxes of pasta and other handy meal-makers. If you pick up 2 to 3 items whenever they're on sale, you'll have a full pantry in no time at all.

Linda's Southern Corn Casserole

Linda Dayringer
Lenoir City, TN

I like to fix this recipe for Thanksgiving and Christmas.
My family loves this casserole and looks forward to it.

3 eggs
1/2 c. butter, melted and
   slightly cooled
1/4 c. sugar
3 14-3/4 oz. cans
   cream-style corn

3 15-1/4 oz. cans corn, drained
8-1/2 oz. pkg. corn muffin mix
1 c. sour cream
2 T. cornstarch
1 t. vanilla extract

Beat eggs in a large bowl; add melted butter. Stir in sugar and cans of corn until well combined. Add dry muffin mix, sour cream, cornstarch and vanilla; stir until well blended. Spoon mixture into a greased 3-quart casserole dish. Bake, uncovered, at 350 degrees for 90 minutes to 2 hours, until puffed and golden, and a knife tip inserted into the center comes out clean. Makes 16 servings.

Whip up a tasty salad in no time at all! Purchase a bag of mixed salad greens and toss in fresh or dried fruit, chopped nuts and shredded cheese. Top off the salad with a drizzle of raspberry vinaigrette and toss.

Potluck
Sides & Salads

Honey Butter Peas & Carrots
Sherry Sheehan
Evensville, TN

In the late 1960s, our grade school cafeteria had the best honey butter that they served with homemade rolls and oven-baked chicken. I had forgotten about it until I suddenly thought of trying honey butter with veggies. It's delicious!

16-oz. pkg. frozen peas
16-oz. pkg. frozen crinkle-cut
   carrots
2 c. water

1/4 c. butter, melted
1/4 c. honey
1/2 t. salt
1/4 t. pepper

In a large saucepan, combine frozen peas and carrots with water. Bring to a boil over medium heat. Cook for 6 to 8 minutes, stirring occasionally. Drain peas and carrots; return to saucepan. Add remaining ingredients; stir until mixed. Serve immediately. Makes 8 servings.

Autumn Brussels Sprouts
Gladys Kielar
Whitehouse, OH

A scrumptious way to dress up Brussels sprouts.

16-oz. pkg. frozen Brussels
   sprouts
10-oz. pkg. frozen peas
2 T. butter

2 stalks celery, chopped
2 slices bacon, crisply cooked
   and crumbled
2 T. fresh chives, minced

Separately cook Brussels sprouts and peas according to package directions; drain and set aside. In a large skillet, melt butter over medium heat. Add celery; cook and stir until tender-crisp. Add Brussels sprouts, peas, crumbled bacon and chives to skillet; toss to combine. Makes 6 servings.

Fall Cooking
with Family & Friends

Winning Baked Beans

*Marsha Baker
Pioneer, OH*

These beans have a deep glaze and rich flavor. I won the "People's Choice Award" at a local Bean Days contest with this recipe! It makes plenty for get-togethers with friends...be prepared to share copies of the recipe.

8 to 10 slices bacon, divided
1 c. yellow or sweet onion,
   chopped
1 to 2 T. butter
5 15-oz. cans pork & beans

3/4 c. catsup
1/4 to 1/2 c. brown sugar,
   packed, to taste
1/3 c. molasses
3 T. mustard

In a skillet over medium heat, cook 4 to 5 bacon slices until crisp; drain on paper towels and crumble. Meanwhile, in another skillet over medium heat, sauté onion in butter until tender. In a large bowl, combine crumbled bacon, onion and remaining ingredients; stir until well blended. Spoon into a 13"x9" baking pan coated with non-stick vegetable spray. Top with remaining, uncooked bacon slices to cover beans. Place pan on center rack of oven. Bake, uncovered, at 325 degrees for 2 to 3 hours, until bubbly, dark and beautifully glazed. Serve warm. Makes 12 servings.

Host a backyard fire pit weenie roast when the weather turns cool and crisp. Serve up Winning Baked Beans and simmering spiced cider... toast marshmallows for dessert. Sure to warm hearts as well as hands!

Potluck
Sides & Salads

Baked Chile-Cheese Rice

Shannon Molden
Hermiston, OR

I developed this recipe and serve it often with grilled flank steak or chicken.

10-oz. can diced tomatoes with
  green chiles
1-1/2 c. water
1 c. cooked rice
1 T. chicken bouillon granules
1 c. sour cream

4-1/2 oz. can chopped
  green chiles
1 t. ground cumin or adobo
  seasoning
2 c. shredded Cheddar Jack
  cheese, divided

Combine tomatoes with juice, water, rice and bouillon in a large saucepan. Bring to a boil over medium-high heat, stirring well to prevent sticking. Reduce heat to medium-low; cover and cook for about 10 minutes, until rice is tender. Stir in sour cream, chiles, cumin or adobo seasoning and 1-1/2 cups cheese. Spoon mixture into a greased 2-quart casserole dish; sprinkle with remaining cheese. Bake, uncovered, at 350 degrees for 35 minutes, or until bubbly and cheese starts to turn golden around the edges. Makes 6 to 8 servings.

For an autumn centerpiece that only takes a moment, place a pumpkin on a cake stand and tuck some bittersweet sprigs around it. Simple yet so eye-catching.

Fall Cooking
with Family & Friends

Best Cheesy Potatoes

Karen Suvak
Galena, OH

These potatoes are almost sinfully good! My nieces & nephews request this recipe at most of our family gatherings. Goes well with holiday ham and all the fixings...great for summer barbecues too!

30-oz. pkg. frozen diced
   hashbrown potatoes
10-3/4 oz. can cream of chicken
   soup
1 to 2 8-oz. pkgs. shredded
   Cheddar cheese

16-oz. container sour cream
2 t. sweet onion, chopped
1 t. salt
1/4 t. pepper
2 c. corn flake cereal, crushed
1/4 c. butter, melted

In a large bowl, combine all ingredients except cereal and butter; stir well. Spread in a lightly greased 13"x9" baking pan. Combine crushed corn flakes and melted butter; top potatoes with mixture. Bake, uncovered, at 350 degrees for one hour, or until bubbly and golden. Makes 10 to 12 servings.

Hard-skinned winter squash cooks in a jiffy in the microwave. Place a halved, seeded squash cut-side down in a microwave-safe dish. Microwave on high until tender and easily pierced..about 6 to 8 minutes for acorn squash, or 10 to 13 minutes for butternuts. Top with butter and spices...yum!

Sides & Salads

Harvest Potatoes

Leticia Janssens
Conroe, TX

This recipe is a delicious, buttery addition to any meal. It's hard not to come back for seconds! Your family will be asking for this again and again.

8 to 10 redskin potatoes, divided
3/4 c. chilled butter, divided
kosher salt and pepper to taste

2 c. shredded Colby Jack cheese, divided
1 c. milk, divided

With a mandoline slicer or a thin, sharp knife, slice 2 to 2-1/2 potatoes; layer in a greased 13"x9" baking pan. Grate 1/4 of chilled butter over potatoes. Season with salt and pepper; add 1/2 cup cheese and 1/4 cup milk. Repeat layering 3 more times. Cover with aluminum foil. Bake at 350 degrees for 45 minutes. Remove foil; bake another 30 minutes. Remove from oven; let stand for 15 minutes and serve. Serves 8.

Cheddar Potato & Gravy Bake

Sharon Crider
Junction City, KS

These potatoes are easy and delicious! I've used this recipe for years.

4 baking potatoes, peeled, sliced
and divided
1/2 c. onion, chopped

10-1/2 oz. can chicken gravy
paprika to taste
1 c. shredded Cheddar cheese

Layer half of potatoes in a greased 2-quart shallow casserole dish. Top with onion and remaining potatoes; spoon gravy over all. Sprinkle with paprika. Cover and bake at 350 degrees for one hour. Uncover; top with cheese. Bake, uncovered, an additional 15 minutes, or until potatoes are tender and cheese is melted. Serves 6.

Fall Cooking
with *Family & Friends*

Our Favorite Green Salad

Lynnette Jones
East Flat Rock, NC

*This salad is extra-special year 'round. Be sure to
use real maple syrup, not pancake syrup!*

4 c. spring mix greens
4 c. romaine lettuce, chopped
1/2 c. candied pecans, chopped
1/2 c. dried cranberries
1 pear or apple, peeled, cored
 and diced
1 c. crumbled Gorgonzola cheese

Combine all ingredients except cheese in a bowl. Pour desired amount
of Dressing over salad and toss. Top with cheese crumbles and serve.
Makes 8 to 10 servings.

Dressing:

1/4 c. olive oil
1 T. Dijon mustard
1 T. pure maple syrup
1 t. cider vinegar

Combine all ingredients in a small jar; add lid and shake well to mix.

The simplest table decorations are often the prettiest!
Fill a rustic wooden bowl with shiny red apples or fragrant
yellow lemons for the kitchen table.

Rick's Requested Macaroni Salad

Sandra Parker
Glen Burnie, MD

I made this for my son on a special family day he had with his friends...they all loved it! Now it's requested whenever he has company coming, which is often.

16-oz. pkg. elbow macaroni,
  uncooked
1-1/2 stalks celery, diced
1/3 c. green pepper, minced
2 medium whole dill pickles,
  diced

3 eggs, hard-boiled, peeled
  and divided
1-1/2 c. mayonnaise
1 t. celery seed
1 t. salt
1/2 t. cracked pepper

Cook macaroni according to package directions, just until tender. Drain; rinse in cold water and drain again. In a large bowl, combine macaroni, celery, green pepper and pickles. Chop 2 eggs and add along with mayonnaise; fold gently. Add seasonings; stir gently until combined. Slice remaining egg and arrange on top. Cover and refrigerate at least 4 hours. Makes 8 to 10 servings.

If you're traveling to join family for Thanksgiving, make a trip bag for each of the kids...a special tote bag that's filled with favorite small toys, puzzles and other fun stuff, reserved just for road trips. The miles will speed by much faster!

Fall Cooking
with *Family & Friends*

Ranch Cornbread Salad

Debbi Bender
Salisbury, MD

*This is a very easy recipe. It's great for using leftover veggies,
as I have used green onions instead of red onion and added some
shredded spinach that I had. Any way you make it, it's a crowd-
pleaser...I have never had leftovers.*

8-1/2 oz. pkg. corn muffin mix
10 slices bacon, crisply cooked
   and chopped
2 eggs, hard-boiled, peeled
   and chopped
1/3 c. green pepper, chopped

1/3 c. red onion, chopped
1 tomato, chopped
2 to 3 T. mayonnaise
1-oz. pkg. ranch salad dressing
   mix, divided

Prepare and bake corn muffin mix according to package directions.
Cool; crumble cornbread into a large bowl. Add bacon, eggs, pepper,
onion and tomato. Gently stir in 2 tablespoons mayonnaise; add
remaining mayonnaise as needed for a moister consistency. Sprinkle
with 1/2 package of dressing mix and stir to combine. Add more
dressing mix to your desired taste. Serve immediately, or cover and
chill until serving time. Makes 6 to 8 servings.

Greet visitors with a bountiful farm-style display on the front porch.
Set up a shock of dried cornstalks, then surround with brightly
colored pumpkins and squash.

Cauliflower "Potato" Salad

Bethany Richter
Canby, MN

I've been making this recipe for quite awhile. The first time I made it, I made several changes to make it more "me." Since then, I make it all the time...no matter what time of the year. I get requests to bring it to potlucks and reunions. I even make it just for myself in the middle of winter because I'm hungry for it. It's that good!

1 head cauliflower, trimmed
6 eggs, hard-boiled, peeled
   and diced
1 c. frozen peas
1 c. mayonnaise

2.8-oz. pkg. real bacon bits
1 T. dried, chopped onions
1 T. honey mustard
salt and pepper to taste

Bring a large saucepan of water to a boil over high heat. Add whole head of cauliflower; simmer for about 10 minutes, until fork-tender. (Cauliflower may be steamed instead.) Drain well; cool and cut into bite-size flowerets. Combine cauliflower and remaining ingredients in a large bowl; mix well. Cover and refrigerate for at least 3 hours, or for best flavor, at least a day or more. Makes 9 to 12 servings.

Add a little whimsy to the dinner table with vintage salt & pepper shakers. Look for them at yard sales or bring your grandmother's old shakers out of the cupboard!

Fall Cooking
with *Family & Friends*

German-Style Red Cabbage

Mary Ann Dell
Phoenixville, PA

A tasty dish to bring to every family gathering. Delicious with grilled or pan-fried sausages...always a huge hit!

3 T. butter
3 Granny Smith apples, cored
 and chopped
1/2 c. onion, chopped
1 small red cabbage, shredded
1 c. white vinegar

1/2 c. brown sugar, packed
2 t. all-purpose flour
1 t. salt
1/4 t. pepper
1/3 c. dry red wine or apple juice

Melt butter in a large skillet over medium heat. Add apples and onion; sauté for 5 minutes. Add cabbage and vinegar; toss to mix. In a bowl, stir together brown sugar, flour, salt and pepper; sprinkle over mixture in skillet. Add wine or apple juice; cover and reduce heat to medium-low. Simmer, stirring often, for about 35 minutes. Makes 6 servings.

ooompah!

On a sunny autumn day, host a backyard Oktoberfest party!
Toss some brats on the grill to serve in hard rolls, topped with
sauerkraut. Round out the menu with potato salad, homemade
applesauce and German chocolate cake for dessert. Set a festive
mood with polka music...sure to be fun for all!

Cranberry Fluff

Panda Spurgin
Bella Vista, AR

This makes a great side dish for roast turkey, baked ham or roast pork tenderloin. My mother always made this recipe several times during the holidays. I don't know where she got it, but it is a family favorite. A whole bag of fresh cranberries makes 3 cups ground cranberries, so you will have a little extra to make cranberry quick bread for breakfast.

2 c. fresh cranberries, ground
3/4 c. sugar
3 c. mini marshmallows
1 c. pineapple chunks, drained
1 c. apple, cored and chopped
1/2 c. seedless green grapes, halved
1/2 c. chopped pecans
1 c. whipping cream

In a large bowl, mix ground cranberries with sugar. Fold in marshmallows; cover and refrigerate overnight. The next day, fold in fruits and pecans; set aside. In a deep bowl, beat cream with an electric mixer on high speed until soft peaks form; fold into cranberry mixture. Spoon salad into a pretty glass serving bowl. Return to refrigerator until ready to serve. Serves 6 to 8.

Garnish servings of gelatin salad with a dollop of creamy lemon mayonnaise. To 1/2 cup of mayonnaise, add 3 tablespoons each of lemon juice, light cream and powdered sugar. Garnish with curls of lemon zest, if you like.

Fall Cooking
with *Family & Friends*

Andrews Family Green Salad   *Kathy Harrison*
Amarillo, TX

My family used to make this salad for every single holiday. There wasn't a Thanksgiving, Christmas or Easter dinner where it wasn't served. But by the time I was 25, my family had all passed away. It was a few years later that I finally made our special green salad again...and all the wonderful memories came flooding back. I get to carry these memories on with my four young children. I hope it brings your family as much joy as it has mine!

3-oz. pkg. lime gelatin mix
1 c. boiling water
8-oz. pkg. cream cheese,
  softened
11-oz. can crushed pineapple,
  drained

8-oz. container frozen whipped
  topping, thawed
Optional: 3/4 to 1 c. chopped
  walnuts or pecans

In a bowl, combine gelatin mix and boiling water. Stir for 2 minutes, or until gelatin dissolves; set aside. In a large bowl, combine cream cheese and pineapple; blend well. Stir gelatin mixture again to make sure it's all dissolved; add to cream cheese mixture and mix well. Add whipped topping; stir for about 2 minutes. Fold in nuts, if using. Transfer to a serving bowl; cover and refrigerate for at least 4 hours. Makes 8 servings.

Pick up a new-to-you fall fruit like quince, persimmon or pomegranate at a farmstand. Ask the vendors how to prepare them...they're sure to have some tasty suggestions to share.

Grandma's Cranberry Salad

Elisha Nelson
Brookline, MO

This is not your ordinary cranberry salad! Our holidays would not be the same without Grandma's cranberry salad. Five generations have enjoyed this salad and it is still the most-requested dish at our holiday table.

2 3-oz. pkgs. raspberry
   gelatin mix
2 c. boiling water
2 c. cold water
3 oranges, peeled and peel from
   1 orange reserved
2 apples, cored and sliced

16-oz. pkg. frozen cranberries,
   thawed
8-oz. can crushed pineapple
1-1/2 c. sugar
2 c. chopped pecans
2 c. mini marshmallows

In a large bowl, combine gelatin mix and boiling water. Stir for 2 minutes, or until completely dissolved. Stir in cold water; set aside. In a food processor, combine oranges, reserved orange peel, apple slices, cranberries, pineapple and sugar; process until orange peel is finely ground. Fold cranberry mixture and pecans into gelatin mixture. Cover and chill for 8 hours or overnight. At serving time, top with marshmallows. This salad may be kept refrigerated for several days. Makes 10 to 12 servings.

Picture-perfect portions of a favorite gelatin salad are handy
for buffets. Spoon the gelatin mixture into paper muffin liners
and set in a baking pan. Chill until firm, then peel off liners.

Fall Cooking
with *Family & Friends*

Simple Sweet Potatoes & Squash

Angela Pike
Russell Springs, KY

*My grandpa loved sweet potatoes. One night I tossed
this together...it became a family favorite!*

2 sweet potatoes, peeled and cut
    into 1-inch cubes
1 butternut squash, peeled, seeds
    removed and cut into
    1-inch cubes

1/4 c. butter, melted
3 T. honey
1/2 t. cinnamon

In a bowl, toss sweet potatoes and squash with butter and honey.
Spread mixture in a 13"x9" baking pan coated with non-stick vegetable
spray. Sprinkle with cinnamon. Bake, uncovered, at 400 degrees for
25 to 30 minutes, until squash is tender. Serves 4 to 6.

Roasted Squash with Sage

Geneva Rogers
Gillette, WY

A flavorful new twist on baked winter squash.

2 acorn or delicata squash,
    halved and seeds removed
1/4 c. butter, softened

1/2 t. salt
1/4 t. pepper
10 fresh sage leaves

Slice squash halves into 1/2-inch crescents. Arrange in a lightly
greased 13"x9" baking pan. Spread butter over squash; season with
salt and pepper. Arrange sage leaves around squash. Bake, uncovered,
at 400 degrees for 20 to 25 minutes, until squash is fork-tender. Makes
8 servings.

Drizzle salad greens with a quick honey
dressing. Whisk together 1/2 cup balsamic
vinegar, 1/4 cup honey, 1/4 cup olive oil and
one teaspoon soy sauce until smooth.

Dinner with Family & Friends

Fall Cooking
with *Family & Friends*

Honey Garlic Stir-Fry Pasta

Cheryl Nidd
Ontario, Canada

This back-to-school dinner favorite is a perfect "switch-up" recipe. No chicken on hand? Use sliced beef or pork! No rigatoni pasta? Use another kind of pasta...even ramen noodles will work, if you're in a hurry. All veggie choices are optional. If you don't like something listed, simply omit it!

2 c. rigatoni pasta, uncooked
1 T. olive oil
2 boneless, skinless chicken
   breasts, cut into strips
8-oz. can sliced water chestnuts,
   drained
1 c. onion, sliced

1 c. broccoli flowerets
1 c. cauliflower flowerets
1 green pepper, sliced
1 red pepper, sliced
6 mushrooms, sliced
3/4 to 1 c. bottled honey-garlic
   sauce

Cook pasta according to package directions; drain. Meanwhile, drizzle a skillet with olive oil; add chicken strips and cook until done. Add all vegetables; cook until vegetables are crisp-tender. Stir in desired amount of sauce; add cooked pasta and toss to mix. Makes 4 to 6 servings.

Dress up a package of brown & serve dinner rolls! Brush
unbaked rolls with a little beaten egg; sprinkle with
sesame seed and bake as directed.

Dinner with Family & Friends

Savory Sausage & Potato Supper

Virginia Campbell
Clifton Forge, VA

This delicious and hearty harvest supper is even more satisfying when served with a simple green salad and buttery garlic bread.

1/4 c. honey mustard
2 T. brown sugar, packed
1 c. dry white wine or chicken
  broth
1 lb. Kielbasa sausage, cut into
  1-inch pieces

4 redskin potatoes, cut into
  3/4-inch cubes
4 carrots, peeled and cut into
  1/2-inch chunks
1 onion, sliced

In a small bowl, stir mustard, brown sugar and wine or broth until well blended; set aside. In a large bowl, combine remaining ingredients. Drizzle with mustard mixture; toss to coat. Spoon mixture into a lightly greased 13"x9" baking pan, scraping all of mustard mixture into pan. Cover with aluminum foil. Bake at 400 degrees for 55 minutes, or until vegetables are tender, stirring occasionally. Serves 4.

Even the simplest meal is special when shared. Why not invite a dinner guest or two, the next time you have a tasty dinner simmering in the slow cooker? The menu doesn't need to be fancy...it's all about food and friendship!

119

Fall Cooking
with *Family & Friends*

Daddy Jack Casserole

Elisha Nelson
Brookline, MO

This recipe was shared by my husband's best friend's mom. In our younger days, she would have this hot and ready for us after a long float trip on the river or a fun snow day. Now we love making this comfort dish for our son! It's delicious served with freshly baked biscuits.

8-oz. pkg. wide egg noodles,
   uncooked
1 lb. ground beef
1 onion, chopped
salt and pepper to taste
10-3/4 oz. can cream of
   mushroom soup

15-1/4 oz. can corn, drained
2-oz. jar diced pimentos, drained
8-oz. pkg. shredded Cheddar
   cheese
2 to 3 T. milk

Cook noodles according to package directions; drain. Meanwhile, in a skillet over medium heat, brown beef and onion. Drain; season with salt and pepper. In a large bowl, combine beef mixture, cooked noodles, mushroom soup, corn, pimentos and cheese; gently fold all ingredients together. Add enough milk to moisten mixture; spoon into a greased 13"x9" baking pan. Bake, uncovered, at 350 degrees for 30 to 45 minutes, until hot and bubbly. Makes 6 servings.

Casseroles are ideal for toting to neighborhood block parties. You'll enjoy catching up with friends while the kids race around playing games. You might even want to set up a table for face painting...so much fun!

Dinner with
Family & Friends

Family Night Iron Skillet
Chicken

Sharon Denise Jones
Fountain, FL

*This is my go-to baked chicken supper. The flavor is rich
and savory...it is never dry and we love it!*

1/4 c. brown sugar, packed
2 T. paprika
1 T. garlic powder
1 T. onion powder
1 T. dried thyme
1 t. chili powder
1/2 t. salt
3 lbs. boneless, skinless
    chicken thighs
1/4 c. butter, melted

In a large plastic zipping bag, combine all ingredients except chicken
and butter. Add chicken; seal bag and turn until pieces are well coated.
Arrange chicken in a cast-iron skillet; drizzle with melted butter. Bake,
uncovered, at 425 degrees for 25 to 30 minutes, until golden and
chicken juices run clear when pierced. Makes 3 to 5 servings.

Start a Thanksgiving tradition. Lay a blank card on each dinner plate
and invite guests to write down what they are most thankful for
this year. Later, bind the cards together with a ribbon to create
a sweet gratitude book.

Fall Cooking
with Family & Friends

Turkey Enchilada Skillet

Connie Hilty
Pearland, TX

My family loves the roast turkey on Thanksgiving, but gets tired of leftovers served the same ol' way. When I found this recipe, I knew it was perfect for jazzing it up! Just add some warm tortillas or a basket of tortilla chips and dinner is served.

2 T. olive oil
1/2 c. onion, chopped
1/2 c. red pepper, chopped
2 cloves garlic, chopped
2 16-oz. jars red or green salsa
15-1/2 oz. can black beans,
    drained and rinsed

8-3/4 oz. can corn, drained
2 c. cooked turkey or chicken,
    cubed
2 c. cooked rice
salt and pepper to taste
1 to 2 c. shredded Mexican-blend
    cheese

Heat oil in a large skillet over medium heat; add onion, red pepper and garlic. Cook for 2 to 3 minutes, stirring occasionally, until onion is nearly tender. Stir in salsa, beans, corn, turkey or chicken and rice. Simmer for 6 to 8 minutes, stirring occasionally. Season with salt and pepper. Remove from heat; sprinkle with cheese. Cover and let stand for several minutes, until cheese is melted. Serves 6 to 8.

Greet your guests with a whimsical pumpkin tower on the
front porch. Arrange pumpkins and squash in graduated sizes
in a stack, using skewers to hold them in place. Clever!

Dinner with Family & Friends

Eva's Chile Pie

Joan Chance
Houston, TX

If you like Tex-Mex or Southwest-style cooking, you will enjoy this meatless recipe I got from a friend. Just add a chopped salad.

9-inch pie crust, unbaked
1-1/2 c. shredded Monterey
  Jack cheese
4-oz. can chopped green chiles,
  drained

1 c. shredded Cheddar cheese
3 eggs, beaten
1/2 c. milk
salt and pepper to taste

Bake pie crust at 400 degrees for 5 minutes; remove from oven. Layer in crust as follows: Monterey Jack cheese, chiles and Cheddar cheese. In a bowl, whisk eggs with milk, salt and pepper; pour over cheese in crust. Bake, uncovered, at 350 degrees for 35 minutes, or until set. Cut into wedges. Serves 6 to 8.

Cheesy Chili Casserole

Deanna Sanford
Indianapolis, IN

Comfort food from childhood! This was the first recipe I learned how to make. My mom helped me with the oven. I love this on cold rainy nights, plus it's so easy to toss together after a long day.

2 14-1/2 oz. cans chili
15-1/4 oz. can corn
8-oz. pkg. shredded Cheddar
  cheese

1 to 1-1/2 c. tortilla chips,
  crushed

Layer chili, corn and cheese in a greased 8"x8" baking pan. Top with crushed tortilla chips. Bake, uncovered, at 350 degrees for 20 minutes, or until heated through and cheese is melted. Serves 4.

Fall Cooking
with *Family & Friends*

Pub-Style Pork Chops

Shirley Howie
Foxboro, MA

A good crusty bread and a tossed salad are all that's needed to round out this full-flavored pub-style meal. I like to use stout beer for this recipe, as it imparts a deep, rich flavor.

4 boneless pork loin chops,
   1/2-inch thick
2 T. oil
1 c. regular or non-alcoholic
   dark beer
2 c. parsnips, peeled and sliced
   1/2-inch thick

2 c. sliced mushrooms
2 cloves garlic, minced
1 T. brown sugar, packed
1 T. Dijon mustard
1/4 t. salt
1/8 t. pepper
Optional: cooked rice

In a large skillet over medium-high heat, brown pork chops in hot oil for 8 to 10 minutes, turning once, until juices run clear. Remove pork chops to a plate; cover to keep warm. Drain skillet; add remaining ingredients except optional rice. Stir to combine. Bring just to boiling; reduce heat to medium-low. Simmer, uncovered, for about 15 minutes, until liquid is reduced to desired consistency and vegetables are tender. Return pork chops to skillet; cover and cook for about 5 minutes more, until heated through. Serve with cooked rice, if desired. Makes 4 servings.

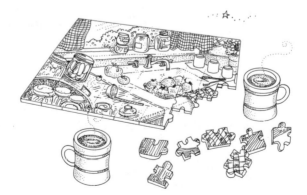

Family night! Serve a simple supper, then spend the evening playing favorite board games or assembling jigsaw puzzles together.

Dinner with Family & Friends

Versatile Baked Pork

Linda Diepholz
Lakeville, MN

This recipe originally called for pork chops...I find it's equally delicious with pork steaks or chicken. I've been making it for years...we have it at least twice a month and never get tired of it! This is delicious with mashed potatoes and steamed broccoli.

2 eggs
1/4 c. all-purpose flour
2 c. Italian-seasoned panko
  crumbs
6 bone-in pork chops or chicken
  pieces, or 2 large pork steaks

salt and pepper to taste
1/4 c. olive oil
10-3/4 oz. can cream of
  mushroom soup
1/2 c. milk
1/3 c. white wine or water

Beat eggs in a shallow bowl; place flour and panko crumbs in separate shallow bowls. Season meat with salt and pepper; coat in flour, dip in egg and coat generously with bread crumbs. Heat oil in a skillet over medium-high heat. Add meat; cook for 5 minutes per side, or until breading is golden. Transfer meat to a greased 13"x9" baking pan; cover with aluminum foil. Bake at 350 degrees for one hour; remove from oven. Whisk together remaining ingredients in a bowl; spoon over meat. Cover again with foil and bake an additional 30 minutes. Makes 6 servings.

Try a ridged cast-iron grill pan for browning pork chops and chicken. It gives a just-grilled look and goes from stovetop to oven with ease.

Fall Cooking
with Family & Friends

Chicken Spaghetti

Lanita Anderson
Lake Lure, NC

This recipe is comfort food at its greatest! My mother made this when I was growing up and it was a favorite of our family. When I married, I tweaked the recipe and it's become one of my family's favorite meals. Served with a crisp salad and hot rolls. Leftovers are delicious too... if there are leftovers!

1 to 2 lbs. boneless, skinless
   chicken breasts
16-oz. pkg. spaghetti, uncooked
1/2 c. onion, chopped
1/2 c. green pepper, chopped
2 stalks celery, chopped
1 clove garlic, minced

1/2 c. butter
10-3/4 oz. cream of chicken soup
10-3/4 oz. can cream of
   mushroom soup
2 c. milk
1/2 t. dried oregano
pepper to taste

In a large saucepan, cover chicken with water. Bring to a boil over high heat; reduce heat to medium-low and simmer until tender. Drain; chop or shred chicken and set aside. Meanwhile, cook spaghetti according to package directions; drain and set aside. In a large skillet over medium heat, sauté onion, green pepper, celery and garlic in butter until crisp-tender. Add cooked chicken, soups, milk and seasonings to mixture in skillet; stir well and heat through. Combine with cooked spaghetti; mix well and spoon into a greased 13"x9" baking pan. Bake, uncovered, at 350 degrees for 20 to 25 minutes, until hot and bubbly. Serves 6 to 8.

Serve fresh-baked muffins and rolls tumbling out of a wicker cornucopia basket...it'll double as a buffet decoration.

Dinner with Family & Friends

Fresh & Quick Tomato Pasta

Rebecca Etling
Blairsville, PA

This has always been my favorite quick meal for hot summer evenings...it's equally good for balmy autumn nights.

2 to 3 ripe tomatoes or 4 to
  6 roma tomatoes, chopped
1/2 to 3/4 lb. fresh mozzarella
  cheese, cut into 1/2-inch
  cubes
3/4 c. fresh basil, cut into
  thin strips
1/2 c. olive oil

1 t. garlic salt
1 t. pepper
1/8 t. red pepper flakes
16-oz. pkg. linguine pasta,
  uncooked
Garnish: 1/2 to 3/4 c. shredded
  Parmesan cheese

Combine all ingredients except pasta and garnish in a bowl. Let stand at room temperature for 30 minutes to allow flavors to blend well. Meanwhile, cook pasta according to package directions; drain. Gently stir tomato mixture into hot pasta until well blended and mozzarella cheese starts to melt. Top with Parmesan cheese; serve immediately. Makes 4 to 6 servings.

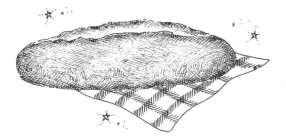

Give garlic bread a Greek twist. Brush a halved loaf of Italian bread with olive oil; sprinkle with lemon-pepper, oregano and garlic. Top with feta cheese and sliced Kalamata olives...broil until hot and bubbly. Delicious!

Fall Cooking
with Family & Friends

Mom's Sparerib Supper

Alice Schnelle
Oak Lawn, IL

This is a fantastic one-pot meal. I have fond memories of my mom cooking these spareribs for dinner. She knew I liked them so much... I think she enjoyed cooking it for that reason.

4-3/4 c. water, divided
3-lb. slab pork spareribs, cut
    into serving-size portions
salt and pepper to taste
1/2 head cabbage, chopped

2 russet potatoes, peeled
    and diced
1/2 c. onion, chopped
14-1/2 oz. can diced tomatoes

Pour 3 cups water into a 5-quart slow cooker. Season spareribs with salt and pepper; arrange in slow cooker. Arrange vegetables around spareribs; season again. Combine undrained tomatoes with remaining water; pour over all. Cover and cook on high setting for 6 to 8 hours, until ribs are falling off the bone and and vegetables are tender. Makes 4 servings.

Get a head start on dinner by peeling and cutting up potatoes the night before. They won't turn dark if you cover them with water before refrigerating them.

Dinner with
Family & Friends

Easy Autumn Pork Roast

Shirley Howie
Foxboro, MA

This is a wonderful roast for entertaining, as it is so easy to prepare. Once it's in the oven, I am free to prepare side dishes and spend time with my guests. Mashed potatoes go really well with this roast, to soak up all the rich, yummy juices!

3 to 4-lb. pork shoulder roast
1/3 c. Worcestershire sauce
1/2 c. apple cider or water
3/4 c. light brown sugar, packed

1 t. dried thyme
1/2 t. pepper
1 t. salt

Preheat oven to 400 degrees. Place pork roast in an ungreased roasting pan; drizzle with Worcestershire sauce. Pour cider or water into pan. Combine brown sugar, thyme and pepper in a bowl; pat mixture over roast to coat. Place uncovered roast in oven; immediately reduce oven temperature to 250 degrees. Bake for 4 hours, or until a meat thermometer inserted in the thickest part reads 160 degrees. Remove roast to a platter; tent with aluminum foil and let stand for 10 minutes. Season pan juices with salt; serve with sliced pork. Serves 6 to 8.

Cranberry-Onion Pork Roast

Sarah Cameron
Fort Belvoir, VA

A slow-cooked sensation! Serve with wild rice mix and a tossed salad for an easy and delicious meal.

2 to 3-lb. boneless pork roast
1.35-oz. pkg. onion soup mix

15-oz. can whole-berry
cranberry sauce

Place pork roast in a 4-quart slow cooker; set aside. Mix together soup mix and cranberry sauce; spoon over roast. Cover and cook on high setting for 6 to 8 hours. Makes 4 to 6 servings.

Place thick slices of onion under a roast for extra flavor...they'll also form a natural rack to keep the roast from cooking in its own fat.

Fall Cooking
with Family & Friends

Garden Taco Rice

Leona Krivda
Belle Vernon, PA

I have been making this for years & my whole family loves it. It's simple, easy and tasty. Ground turkey may be used instead of beef, if you prefer. Serve with a side salad and some garlic toast for a great meal.

1 to 1-1/2 lbs. ground beef
salt and pepper to taste
1/4 c. onion, finely minced
16-oz. jar picante sauce
1-1/2 c. water
1-1/4 oz. pkg. taco seasoning
   mix
14-1/2 oz. can stewed tomatoes
1-1/2 c. zucchini, thinly sliced

1 c. black beans, drained
   and rinsed
1 c. corn
garlic powder to taste
1-1/2 c. instant rice, uncooked
1 c. shredded Cheddar cheese
Garnish: sour cream, additional
   picante sauce and shredded
   cheese

Brown beef in a large skillet over medium heat. Drain well; season lightly with salt and pepper. Add onion; cook and stir just until softened. Stir in remaining ingredients except rice, cheese and garnish; bring to a boil. Reduce heat to low; stir in rice. Cover and simmer for 5 to 7 minutes, until liquid is absorbed, stirring occasionally. Remove from heat; fluff with a fork and top with cheese. Cover and let stand for 3 minutes, until cheese melts. Garnish as desired. Makes 4 to 6 servings.

Prefer to shred cheese yourself? Freeze the wrapped block of cheese for 15 minutes...it will just glide across the grater!

Dinner with
Family & Friends

Easy Hungarian Goulash

Brenda Bodnar
Mayfield Village, OH

This warm, fragrant stew fills the house with delicious aromas and melts in your mouth at dinnertime. Add a tossed green salad and you're good to go. Leftovers heat well in the microwave and make great lunches to take to work. Your co-workers will be envious!

2 T. butter
1 T. oil
2 lbs. onions, thinly sliced
2 lbs. stew beef cubes
1/4 c. sweet paprika

1-1/2 t. salt
8-oz. container sour cream
4 c. hot cooked egg noodles,
    buttered

Melt butter with oil in a large Dutch oven or deep skillet over medium-high heat. Cook onions until lightly golden. Add beef; sprinkle with paprika and salt. Cook for about 2 minutes, until beef is heated through. Reduce heat to low. Cover and simmer for 1-1/2 to 2 hours until beef is tender, stirring occasionally. Add a little water if it gets too dry. Stir in sour cream and heat through; be careful not to boil. Serve over buttered noodles. Serves 8.

Hosting family dinner on Thanksgiving? Ask everyone to bring a baby photo. Post them on a big board and have a contest... the first person to guess who's who gets a prize!

Fall Cooking
with *Family & Friends*

Pot Roast with Gravy

Sandra Mirando
Depew, NY

My husband always said he never liked pot roast until he tasted this one. It is delicious and very easy. I serve this with mashed potatoes.

3-lb. beef chuck roast
salt and pepper to taste
2 T. canola oil
4 onions, quartered and divided
1.1-oz. pkg. beefy onion
   soup mix

1-1/2 c. hot water
6 carrots, peeled and cut
   into chunks
3 T. all-purpose flour
1/4 c. cold water

Pat both sides of roast dry with paper towel; season both sides with salt and pepper. Heat oil in a large Dutch oven over medium-high heat. Add roast and brown on both sides. Add one onion to pan; continue to brown. Dissolve soup mix in hot water. Pour 3/4 cup of mixture around roast; bring to a boil. Cover and bake at 325 degrees for 60 minutes. Arrange carrots and remaining onions around roast. Cover and bake for an additional 60 to 75 minutes, until roast is fork-tender. Remove roast and vegetables to a platter; set pan on stovetop. Add remaining soup mixture to drippings in pan, to equal 3 cups. Combine flour and cold water in a small jar; shake well and gradually stir into drippings. Cook over medium heat, stirring constantly, until mixture thickens and boils. Serve gravy with roast and vegetables. Serves 6.

Slow-cooked beef chuck roast is always a winner! Any leftovers will be equally delicious in sandwiches, soups or casseroles, so be sure to choose a large roast even if your family is small.

Italian Meatloaf

Mary Brassilio
Sioux City, IA

This was my grandmother's recipe...it's perfect comfort food for a family meal together.

1 lb. ground beef
1 lb. Italian-seasoned ground
   pork sausage
2 eggs, beaten
2-1/2 c. Italian-seasoned dry
   bread crumbs, or 6 pieces
   dry bread, crushed
3 T. grated Parmesan cheese

1 T. dried parsley
1 clove garlic, pressed
1 t. dried oregano
1 t. salt
1/4 c. catsup
1/4 c. brown sugar, packed
1 T. mustard

In a large bowl, mix together all ingredients except catsup, brown sugar and mustard. Mix well and press gently into a lightly greased 8"x8" glass baking pan. In a small bowl, mix remaining ingredients; spread over beef mixture. Bake, uncovered, at 350 degrees for onc hour. Makes 6 servings.

For an easy weeknight dinner or perfect party fare, just combine one pound frozen meatballs, one jar spaghetti sauce and one cup water in a slow cooker. Cover and cook on low setting for 6 to 8 hours. Serve meatballs on toasted rolls, topped with shredded mozzarella cheese. Yum!

Fall Cooking
with *Family & Friends*

Andy's Garlic Butter Shrimp

Tiffany Jones
Batesville, AR

My husband Andy and my daughter Elizabeth love shrimp. I've always been nervous about cooking shrimp myself, but this was a major hit! They like to eat it over buttered spaghetti noodles.

1 lb. frozen uncooked large
    shrimp with tails, thawed
    and peeled
1 T. garlic powder
1/2 t. Creole seasoning
salt and pepper to taste

1 c. butter
1/2 c. chicken broth
1 t. smoked paprika
Optional: hot cooked spaghetti,
    buttered

Place shrimp in a bowl; sprinkle with seasonings and set aside. Melt butter in a large skillet over medium heat. Add shrimp to skillet; cook over medium-high heat for 10 minutes. Add chicken broth and paprika to skillet; continue cooking for 5 minutes. Remove shrimp to a serving bowl. Serve with broth mixture in skillet spooned over cooked spaghetti, or enjoy shrimp on its own. Makes 4 servings.

Gourds and mini pumpkins left over from Halloween can do double duty on the Thanksgiving table. Spray them gold with craft paint and tuck into harvest centerpieces.

Dinner with
Family & Friends

Doreen's Crab Cakes

Doreen Knapp
Stanfordville, NY

*I love these crab cakes, served with lots of fresh lemon juice
and my scrumptious Homemade Tartar Sauce.*

1/2 c. panko crumbs
1 lb. fresh crabmeat, flaked
2 T. mayonnaise
1 T. grainy mustard
1 egg, beaten
1/2 t. dried parsley

1/4 t. celery seed
1/2 t. salt
1/4 t. pepper
1 to 2 T. butter
Garnish: lemon wedges

Make Homemade Tartar Sauce ahead of time; refrigerate. Put panko
crumbs in a shallow bowl; set aside. In a bowl, combine remaining
ingredients except butter and garnish; shape into 3-inch inch patties.
Coat both sides of patties in crumbs. In a large skillet, melt butter over
medium heat. Add patties; cook until golden on both sides. Drain on a
paper towel-lined plate. Serve crab cakes with fresh lemon wedges and
tartar sauce. Makes 6 servings.

Homemade Tartar Sauce:

1 c. mayonnaise
1-1/2 T. gherkin pickles, finely
   chopped
1 T. shallot or red onion,
   chopped
1 T. fresh parsley, chopped

1 t. cracked pepper
1 t. Dijon mustard
1 to 2 t. lemon juice
Optional: 1 t. fresh dill weed
   or tarragon, minced

Combine all ingredients, adding lemon juice to taste; mix well. For best
flavor, refrigerate overnight. Makes about one cup.

Mix up some pineapple coleslaw! Combine
a package of shredded coleslaw mix and
your favorite coleslaw dressing, adding
dressing to taste. Stir in drained
pineapple tidbits for a sweet twist.

Fall Cooking
with *Family & Friends*

Sauerkraut & Meatballs

Goldie White
Greenville, OH

Every get-together I go to, I'm required to bring this dish. Most people love it because it's different, and it isn't sour from the sauerkraut.

2 lbs. ground beef
3 eggs, beaten
1 c. fine dry bread crumbs
1.35-oz. pkg. onion soup mix
2 14-1/2 oz. cans sauerkraut,
   drained and divided

15-oz. can jellied cranberry
   sauce
2/3 c. barbecue sauce
1 c. brown sugar, packed

In a large bowl, combine beef, eggs, bread crumbs and soup mix. Mix well and shape into golfball-size balls; set aside. Spread one can of sauerkraut in a greased 13"x9" baking pan. Arrange meatballs on top of sauerkraut; spread remaining can of sauerkraut over meatballs. Combine cranberry sauce, barbecue sauce and brown sugar in a bowl; mix well and spoon over sauerkraut. Bake, uncovered, at 350 degrees for one hour, or until meatballs are cooked through. Serves 8 to 10.

Have everyone bundle up in their merriest mittens, hats and coats and go outdoors! While everyone's home, it's the perfect time to take photos for this year's Christmas cards.

Dinner with
Family & Friends

Pineapple Kielbasa over Rice
Andria Meyers
Chester, MT

This is a go-to recipe for our family for a quick & easy weeknight dinner, especially when we have activities or limited time. It's so simple, but so delicious! Add a bagged salad mix or a quick vegetable on the side and dinner is ready in a flash. It's an any-season meal that the whole family loves!

1 lb. Kielbasa sausage, cut into
   1-inch pieces
Optional: 2 to 3 t. oil
1/2 t. garlic powder

salt and pepper to taste
20-oz. can pineapple tidbits
1 T. dried, minced onions
cooked rice

Sauté sausage in a skillet over medium-high heat until browned, adding oil if desired. Drain; sprinkle with seasonings. Spoon pineapple with juice over sausage; sprinkle with onions. Reduce heat to medium-low. Simmer, uncovered, until juice is evaporated. Serve over cooked rice. Makes 4 to 6 servings.

Chicken Jax
Tracee LaRose
British Columbia, Canada

This is one of my special-needs son Jaxon's favorite ways to eat chicken. Our whole family enjoys it as well and it is quick & easy.

1 T. oil
4 to 6 boneless, skinless
   chicken breasts, each sliced
   into 3 pieces
1 t. garlic powder

salt and pepper to taste
7-1/2 oz. container garlic &
   herb cream cheese
1/4 c. milk

Heat oil in a large skillet over medium-high heat; add chicken and seasonings. Cook for 6 to 7 minutes per side, until cooked through. Reduce heat to medium; stir in cream cheese and milk. Simmer for about 5 minutes, until heated through. Makes 4 to 6 servings.

Fall Cooking
with *Family & Friends*

Favorite Roast Turkey

Stephanie Dardani-D'Esposito
Ravena, NY

This is how I cook my turkey every Thanksgiving.
It turns out delicious every time!

13 to 15-lb. turkey, thawed
   if frozen
1/2 c. plus T. salt, divided
2 stalks celery, cut into chunks
1 onion, quartered
2 T. olive oil

3 T. garlic powder
3 T. onion powder
1 T. pepper
12-oz. bottle regular or
   non-alcoholic light beer

Unwrap turkey. Remove neck and giblets; use for another purpose or discard. Place turkey in a roasting pan, breast-side up. Put 1/2 cup of salt into the cavity; place celery and onion inside cavity. Pat turkey dry with a paper towel. Rub with olive oil; sprinkle with remaining salt and other seasonings. Pour beer into the cavity; beer will fill the pan. Cover loosely with aluminum foil. Bake at 350 degrees for 2 hours. Uncover and bake for another one to 1-1/2 hours, until a meat thermometer inserted in the thickest part of breast reads 170 degrees. Remove from oven; cover loosely with foil and let stand for 30 to 45 minutes. Carve and serve. Serves 8.

Hosting a big Thanksgiving gathering? The day before the big day, set out all the serving platters and dishes. Add labels like "Roast Turkey" and "Jane's Pumpkin Muffins." You'll be able to set out dinner in a jiffy!

Dinner with
Family & Friends

Grilled Turkey Tenderloins

Darrell Lawry
Kissimmee, FL

Here in Florida, it's usually in the 70s on Thanksgiving Day!
We have some friends over and I fix these tasty tenderloins and
some veggies on the grill. It's always a festive occasion for us.

1 lb. turkey tenderloins
1/4 c. soy sauce
1/4 c. canola oil
1/4 c. dry sherry or chicken broth
2 T. lemon juice

2 T. dried, minced onions
1/4 t. ground ginger
1/8 t. garlic salt
1/8 t. pepper

Pound or flatten turkey tenderloins to one-inch thickness; set aside.
In a shallow pan, blend together remaining ingredients. Add tenderloins;
turn to coat both sides. Cover and refrigerate for several hours, turning
occasionally. Drain; discard marinade. Grill tenderloins over hot coals,
about 6 to 8 minutes per side, depending on thickness, until no longer
pink in the center. Do not overcook. Let stand several minutes before
serving. Serves 4.

Dan's Poultry Rub

Muriel Vlahakis
Sarasota, FL

This special spice rub makes chicken a holiday meal, anytime!
This is delicious on pork roast, too. I keep this spice rub in a
covered container in the pantry, ready whenever I want it.

2 T. brown sugar, packed
2 T. greens seasoning
2 T. paprika

1 T. pepper
1 t. garlic powder
Optional: 1 T. salt

Mix all ingredients well in a small bowl; store in a covered jar. To use,
pat a roasting chicken dry. Rub with olive oil; coat with poultry rub
and bake as desired. Makes enough for one chicken.

Stock up on take-out containers...perfect for sending home
Turkey Day leftovers with guests.

Fall Cooking
with *Family & Friends*

Pork Chops & Scalloped Corn *Jolene Roberts*
Loraine, IL

My husband's favorite dish! His mother used to make it, and now our children love it too.

6 bone-in pork chops
1 to 2 T. oil
2 eggs, beaten
15-1/4 oz. can corn, drained
14-3/4 oz. can cream-style corn

1 c. milk
1/4 c. butter, melted
1 sleeve saltine crackers,
   crushed
salt and pepper to taste

In a skillet over medium heat, brown pork chops in oil on both sides. Arrange pork chops in a greased 13"x9" baking pan; set aside. Combine remaining ingredients in a bowl; mix well and spoon over pork chops. Cover with aluminum foil. Bake at 350 degrees for one hour. Remove foil during last 15 minutes to allow corn to brown. Makes 6 servings.

Dress up dining room chairs in a snap while directing guests
to their seats...tie a pretty ribbon around the chair back
and tuck in a folded placecard.

Creamed Turkey

Stephanie Nilsen
Fremont, NE

We have used this recipe since the 1960s with our leftover holiday turkey. It can be served over buttered toast or warm, flaky biscuits...so warm and comforting!

2 T. butter, sliced
1/4 c. celery, minced
2 T. all-purpose flour
1/2 t. poultry seasoning
12-oz. can evaporated milk

2 c. cooked turkey, chopped
1 c. peas, thawed if frozen
1 T. chopped pimentos, drained
buttered toast or warm biscuits

Melt butter in the top pan of a double boiler, with water at a rolling boil in bottom pan. Add celery; cook and stir until translucent, about 3 minutes. Combine flour and seasoning in a cup; add to butter mixture. Cook, stirring quickly, until thickened. Stir in evaporated milk, a little at a time. Continue to cook, stirring occasionally, until sauce is thickened. Add turkey, peas and pimentos; cook and stir until heated through. Meanwhile, prepare one to 2 slices buttered toast for each person, or bake and split biscuits. Serve creamed turkey over toast or biscuits. Serves 4.

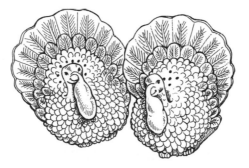

Choosing a holiday turkey? Allow about one pound per person, plus a little extra for leftovers. A 15-pound turkey will serve 12 people, with enough left to enjoy turkey sandwiches, turkey tetrazzini or turkey soup afterwards.

Fall Cooking
with Family & Friends

Spaghetti Bread

Jenifer Rutland
Hiawatha, KS

This easy recipe tastes like spaghetti without the noodles. It's a kid favorite at our house!

1 lb. ground beef
Italian seasoning, salt and
   pepper to taste
16-oz. jar pasta sauce
1 loaf French bread, halved
   lengthwise

2 to 3 T. butter, softened
garlic powder to taste
1 c. shredded Colby & Monterey
   Jack cheese

Brown beef in a skillet over medium heat; drain. Sprinkle with Italian seasoning, salt and pepper as desired; stir in pasta sauce. Bring to a simmer over low heat. Meanwhile, spread cut sides of bread with butter; sprinkle with garlic powder. Place on a baking sheet; bake at 350 degrees for 2 to 3 minutes, just long enough to melt the butter and toast the edges. Remove bread from oven; use a spoon to press down bread in the center and along the edges. (This will help the beef mixture stay on the bread.) Spoon beef mixture onto each half of bread slice; cover with cheese. Bake at 350 degrees for 15 to 25 minutes, until cheese is melted and bread is toasted as desired. Slice to serve. Serves 5.

Pitch a tent in the backyard on a fall night so the kids can camp out, tell ghost stories and play flashlight tag. What a great way to make memories!

Dinner with
Family & Friends

French Bread Pizza

Tiffany Jones
Batesville, AR

My twins Elizabeth and Noah love pizza. My husband Andy is a picky eater. We like to make this together for the family and everyone loves it. So yummy!

1/2 c. butter, softened
1 t. garlic powder
1 t. onion powder
1 loaf French bread, halved
   lengthwise

15-oz. jar pizza sauce
2 c. shredded Italian-blend
   cheese

In a bowl, blend butter and seasonings. Spread butter mixture over cut sides of bread; place on an ungreased baking sheet. Bake at 350 degrees for 10 minutes. Remove from oven; top bread with pizza sauce and cheese. Return to oven and bake an additional 10 minutes, or until hot and bubbly. Cut into slices to serve. Serves 6.

Chili Dogs in a Blanket

Dianne Young
Lehi, UT

We love this recipe for family gatherings. It is a simple meal to prepare and so yummy!

2 16-oz. cans favorite chili,
   divided
1/2 to 1 c. shredded Cheddar
   cheese, divided
6 flour tortillas

6 hot dogs
Garnish: chopped onions,
   tomatoes, black olives,
   lettuce, sour cream

Pour one can of chili into a lightly greased 9"x9" baking pan. Sprinkle a small amount of cheese on each tortilla; add a hot dog and roll up tortilla. Place seam-side down in pan. Top with remaining cheese and chili. Cover pan with aluminum foil. Bake at 425 degrees for 25 minutes, or until hot dogs are heated through and cheese is melted. Garnish as desired and serve. Serves 6.

Fall Cooking
with Family & Friends

Gran's Mac & Cheese

Virginia Campbell
Clifton Forge, VA

Comfort food from Gran herself! She was the best cook ever. It's so hard to wait for this to be cooked and then cool enough to eat, but it's so worth the wait. Everyone was always on their best behavior while this was baking in Gran's kitchen, so they wouldn't be left out. Other kids would come to play at my house in hopes of a treat. This is very filling and satisfying, and it works as either a side dish or a main course.

16-oz. pkg. elbow macaroni, uncooked
16-oz. pkg. shredded sharp Cheddar cheese, or more as desired
2 c. half-and-half or whipping cream

Optional: whole milk as needed
1/2 c. butter, cut into 8 slices
coarse pepper to taste
1 c. grated Parmesan cheese, or more as desired

Cook macaroni according to package directions, just until tender; drain. To a buttered 13"x9" baking pan, add half of cooked macaroni; spread to cover bottom of pan. Top evenly with all of Cheddar cheese. Cover cheese with remaining macaroni, spreading to cover cheese completely. Pour half-and-half or cream over top. (Liquid should come to the top of macaroni and cheese; add some milk, if needed.) Dot with butter; season very lightly with pepper. Top with Parmesan cheese. Cover with aluminum foil. Bake at 350 degrees for 30 minutes. Let stand in covered pan for 10 minutes before serving. Makes 15 servings.

Thanksgiving is so family-centered...why not host a post-holiday potluck with friends later in the weekend? Everyone can bring their favorite "leftover" concoctions, relax and catch up together.

Grilled Marinated Chicken

Jeff Bastian
Millmont, PA

*This is a very special recipe! I came up with the marinade and
we've been using it for chicken and venison ever since. It's delicious!
A great fall meal served with potatoes and tossed salad.*

7 to 8 boneless, skinless chicken
   thighs or 4 boneless, skinless
   chicken breasts
1/4 c. Worcestershire sauce
1/4 c. soy sauce
1/4 c. vinegar

1/4 c. red cooking wine or
   red grape juice
1/4 c. brown sugar, packed
1 t. Cajun seasoning
1 t. pepper

Place chicken in a large bowl; set aside. In another bowl, mix together
remaining ingredients thoroughly, making sure to dissolve brown sugar.
Spoon marinade over chicken; turn to coat well. Cover and refrigerate
about 4 hours, turning chicken several times. Drain and discard
marinade; grill chicken as desired. Serves 4 to 5.

A pat of herb butter makes fresh-baked rolls taste even better.
Blend 1/2 cup softened butter with a teaspoon each of chopped fresh
parsley, dill and chives. Roll into a log or pack into a crock and chill.

El Dorado Casserole

*Mary Scurti
Highland, CA*

*This dish is a favorite whenever we have company for dinner,
or go to a picnic. Serve with a salad and dinner is complete!*

1-1/2 lbs. ground beef or
  ground turkey
salt and pepper to taste
1-1/4 oz. pkg. taco seasoning
  mix
3 8-oz. cans tomato sauce
1 onion, chopped
2-1/4 oz. can chopped
  black olives

1-1/2 c. sour cream
1-1/2 c. cottage cheese
7-oz. can diced green chiles
8-oz. pkg. nacho cheese tortilla
  chips, crushed and divided
8-oz. pkg. shredded Mexican-
  blend cheese
Garnish: additional sour cream

Brown beef or turkey in a large skillet over medium heat. Drain; season
with salt and pepper. Stir in taco seasoning, tomato sauce, onion and
olives; remove from heat. In a bowl, mix sour cream, cottage cheese
and chiles; set aside. Spread half of tortilla chips in a deep 13"x9" baking
pan coated with non-stick vegetable spray. Layer with half each of
beef mixture, sour cream mixture and cheese. Repeat layers. Bake,
uncovered, at 300 degrees for 20 to 30 minutes, or until bubbly and
cheese is melted. Serve with extra sour cream for topping. Serves 6 to 8.

Show your hometown spirit...cheer on the high school football team with
a neighborhood block party. Invite neighbors to bring along their favorite
dish to share...don't forget to add a game of beanbag toss for the kids!

Dinner with
Family & Friends

Authentic Spanish Rice

Bernadette Hoffman
Port Orchard, WA

My family has used this recipe for five generations. My family is Mexican-American, so this is as authentic as you can get! My husband and our children have enjoyed it for many years.

2 T. oil
1 c. long-cooking rice, uncooked
1/2 c. yellow onion, chopped
1/2 green pepper, chopped
1 ripe tomato, chopped

1 t. ground cumin
1 t. garlic powder
1/2 t. salt
8-oz. can tomato sauce
2 c. water

Heat oil in a large skillet over medium heat; add rice, onion, green pepper, tomato and seasonings. Cook, stirring occasionally, until rice is golden and vegetables are tender. Add tomato sauce and water; bring to a boil. Reduce heat to low. Cover and simmer for 15 minutes, or until rice is tender. Makes 4 to 6 servings.

One of the best ways to give thanks is to help someone else.
Volunteer, lend a neighbor a hand, leave a surprise on
someone's doorstep...thoughtful ways to show you care.

Fall Cooking
with *Family & Friends*

Quick Shrimp Creole

*Carol Creel
Garner, NC*

A tasty Creole recipe...for more heat, just add some hot sauce.

1/4 c. onion, chopped
1/4 c. celery, chopped
1/4 c. green pepper, chopped
1 clove garlic, minced
1-1/2 T. oil
8 oz. can tomato sauce
1/2 t. Worcestershire sauce

1/2 t. cornstarch
1/8 t. pepper
1 t. water
3/4 lb. frozen uncooked medium
   shrimp, cleaned
cooked rice

In a skillet over medium heat, sauté vegetables in oil. Add sauces, cornstarch, pepper and water; add frozen shrimp. Cook for about 4 to 5 minutes, until shrimp turn pink. Serve over cooked rice. Makes 2 to 3 servings.

Baked Marinated Halibut

*Jo Ann
Gooseberry Patch*

An easy fish dish we all enjoy...good with salmon too. I like to serve it with cooked rice and a steamed green vegetable.

1/4 c. butter, melted
1/4 c. lemon juice
1/4 c. green onions, sliced
2 T. water

1/2 t. garlic salt
1/4 to 1/2 t. dill weed
1 lb. halibut steaks, thawed
   if frozen

In a greased shallow 13"x9" baking pan, mix all ingredients except fish. Add fish to pan; turn to coat and refrigerate for one hour. Bake fish in marinade, uncovered, at 400 degrees for 10 minutes, or until fish flakes easily with a fork. Serves 2 to 4.

For fresh-tasting fish, place thawed fillets in a shallow dish and cover with milk. Soak for 20 minutes, drain and pat dry.

Dinner with
Family & Friends

Tuna Noodle Casserole

Charlotte Thacker
Wadesville, IN

This recipe was given to me years ago and I adjusted it slightly to suit my family. Since then, it's the only recipe I'll use for Tuna Noodle Casserole. Now my grown daughters use it for their families. I have many Gooseberry Patch cookbooks (I read them like novels!) and have never seen a recipe like this one. It is so good.

6-oz. pkg. egg noodles,
   uncooked
10-3/4 oz. can cream of
   celery soup
1 to 2 5-oz. cans tuna, drained
   and flaked
1 c. mayonnaise
1 c. milk

1/2 t. salt
1/2 c. celery, thinly sliced
1/4 c. shredded Cheddar cheese
1/4 c. shredded American cheese
Optional: 1 c. canned peas,
   drained
Garnish: crushed potato chips

Cook noodles according to package directions; drain. Meanwhile, in a saucepan, mix together remaining ingredients except garnish. Cook over medium heat until well blended and cheese is melted. Fold in cooked noodles; mix gently and transfer to a greased 2-quart casserole dish. Top with crushed potato chips. Bake, uncovered, at 400 degrees for about 50 minutes, until bubbly and potato chips are golden. Serves 4 to 6.

Back to school, tailgating parties, Halloween, Thanksgiving dinner...
autumn is a busy time! Take it easy. Keep a notepad on the fridge
for a running grocery list...no more running to the store
at the last minute before starting dinner.

Fall Cooking
with Family & Friends

Spareribs & Sauerkraut

Peggy Frazier
Indianapolis, IN

This is definitely a comfort meal and one of our family favorites. Our family enjoys this with buttered mashed potatoes, spooning the sauerkraut on top of the mashed potatoes.

6 to 7 lbs. country-style pork loin spareribs, cut into serving-size portions
salt and pepper to taste
3 16-oz. cans sauerkraut, very well drained
1-1/2 c. Granny Smith apples, peeled, cored and chopped
3/4 c. onion, coarsely chopped
8 to 12 whole cloves
1/4 c. brown sugar, packed
1/4 t. pepper
1-1/2 c. chicken broth, or more as needed

Arrange spareribs in a shallow roasting pan; season on all sides with salt and pepper. Broil under a preheated broiler, 6 inches from heat, for 20 to 30 minutes, until ribs are browned on all sides. In a heavy, deep Dutch oven, combine remaining ingredients; stir gently. Arrange ribs on top, pushing them down into sauerkraut mixture. Turn oven to 325 degrees; cover and bake for 2 hours. Baste twice, spooning up pan juices onto ribs. Make sure the liquid does not cook away; if it gets low, add more broth. (This will not be a problem if a heavy pan is used.) Serve sauerkraut mixture alongside ribs. Makes 6 to 8 servings.

Make some Halloween memories! Invite friends to visit, dress up in thrift-shop costumes and take pictures, make popcorn balls together and watch all the old, classic monster movies!

Dinner with Family & Friends

Southwest Turkey Casserole
Betty Kozlowski
Newnan, GA

A great way to enjoy leftover turkey, and it can either be baked or cooked in a slow cooker! Your family will love it.

1 c. cooked turkey, cubed
6 corn tortillas, cut into
  1-inch pieces
10-3/4 oz. can cream of chicken
  soup
4-oz. can chopped green chiles

1/2 c. sour cream or plain yogurt
1 c. corn
1/2 c. onion, chopped
1/2 c. shredded Cheddar cheese,
  divided

In a large saucepan, combine all ingredients except cheese. Cook over medium heat, stirring occasionally, until heated through. Spread half of mixture in a greased 1-1/2 quart casserole dish; top with half of cheese. Repeat layers. Bake, uncovered, at 350 degrees for 20 to 25 minutes, until hot and bubbly. For a slow cooker, omit stovetop step; layer as above in a 4-quart slow cooker. Cover and cook on high setting for one to 2 hours. Makes 4 servings.

Over the river and through the wood,
To grandmother's house we go;
The horse knows the way to carry the sleigh
Through the white and drifted snow.
–Lydia Maria Child

Fall Cooking
with *Family & Friends*

Chili & Cornbread Waffles

Kay Daugherty
Collinsville, MS

This recipe is perfect for Friday night suppers when there is a chill in the air. Let the slow cooker do the cooking while you're at work, then the waffle iron can turn out crisp waffles when you get home. Top with all your favorites like sour cream and shredded cheese, and your comfort meal is on the table! Sure to be a favorite.

1-1/2 lbs. ground beef chuck or
   ground turkey
salt and pepper to taste
14-1/2 oz. can diced tomatoes
15-1/2 oz. can kidney beans,
   drained and rinsed
8-oz. can tomato sauce

6-oz. can tomato paste
1 c. chicken broth
1-1/4 oz. pkg. chili seasoning
   mix
Garnish: sour cream, shredded
   Cheddar cheese, chopped
   green chiles

Brown beef or turkey in a skillet over medium heat, seasoning with salt and pepper. Drain; remove from heat. Spray a 4-quart slow cooker with non-stick vegetable spray. Add tomatoes with juice and remaining ingredients except garnish; stir until well combined. Add beef or turkey and stir again. Cover and cook on low setting for 6 to 8 hours. Shortly before serving time, make Cornbread Waffles. Serve waffles topped with chili; garnish as desired. Makes 4 servings.

Cornbread Waffles:

2 6-oz. pkgs. Mexican-style
   cornbread mix

2 eggs, beaten
1-1/3 c. milk

Combine all ingredients; beat until smooth. Spray preheated waffle iron with non-stick spray. Pour one cup of batter per waffle onto waffle iron; cook according to manufacturer's directions.

Fall Harvest
Party Treats

Fall Cooking
with Family & Friends

Nacho Pie

Jacki Smith
Fayetteville, NC

My mom's friend made this recipe for our family when my sisters and I were growing up. It is one of the first meals we all learned to make, and it's a family favorite, hands down. Great for tailgating or potlucks!

16-oz. can refried beans
1 lb. ground beef
1 onion, chopped
2/3 c. water
1-1/4 oz. pkg. taco seasoning
   mix
4-oz. can chopped green chiles

2-1/4 oz. jar green salad
   olives, drained
2 c. shredded Monterey Jack
   cheese
8-oz. jar taco sauce
Garnish: sour cream,
   tortilla chips

Spread refried beans in a lightly greased 9"x9" baking pan; set aside. In a skillet over medium heat, brown beef with onion; drain. Stir in water and seasoning mix; simmer for several minutes. Stir in chiles and olives; spoon over beans in pan. Top with cheese and taco sauce. Bake, uncovered, at 350 degrees for 35 minutes, or until bubbly and cheese is melted. Serve with sour cream and tortilla chips. Makes 8 servings.

For no-stress entertaining, have an all-appetizers party! Set up tables in different areas so guests can mingle as they enjoy yummy spreads and finger foods. Your get-together is sure to be a scrumptious success.

Fall Harvest Party Treats

Roasted Red Pepper Dip

Lisa Ashton
Aston, PA

*This is a great dip, really good! I've even used my own
roasted peppers to make it.*

12-oz. jar roasted red peppers,
   drained
1-oz. pkg. ranch dip
   seasoning mix

8-oz. pkg. cream cheese,
   softened
sliced baguette bread

Add roasted peppers to a food processor and chop well. Add seasoning
mix and cream cheese; pulse until well blended. Spoon into a bowl;
cover and chill until serving time. Serve with sliced baguette bread.
Serves 8.

White Queso Dip

Liz Plotnick-Snay
Gooseberry Patch

*Serve with your favorite white tortilla chips or
cut-up vegetables...sure to be a big hit!*

32-oz. pkg. pasteurized white
   process cheese, cubed
1/2 c. milk

4-oz. can diced green chiles
1 t. taco seasoning mix

Combine cheese and milk in a large saucepan over medium-low heat.
Cook and stir until cheese is melted and smooth. Remove from heat;
stir in chiles and seasoning mix. Serve hot. May be reheated in the
microwave, stirring after every 30 seconds, until desired consistency.
Makes 10 servings.

Set a pillar candle in a glass globe that's
partially filled with candy corn or fresh
cranberries...it sets a fall mood instantly
for any party table!

Fall Cooking
with *Family & Friends*

Honey-Glazed Wings

Jo Ann
Gooseberry Patch

A tasty use for that local honey you picked up at the farmers' market! Try this easy sauce on boneless, skinless chicken breasts for a tasty main dish.

2 lbs. chicken wings, separated
pepper to taste
1 c. honey
1/2 c. soy sauce

2 T. catsup
2 T. oil
1 clove garlic, pressed

Season wings generously with pepper; arrange in a lightly greased shallow 13"x9" baking pan and set aside. Combine remaining ingredients in a bowl; mix well and spoon over wings. Bake, uncovered, at 350 degrees for 45 minutes, turning wings occasionally, or until sauce has thickened and chicken juices run clear when pierced. Makes 1-1/2 to 2 dozen.

Take advantage of the holiday decorations that fill stores in late autumn. Shiny gold glass balls mix well with natural materials like pine cones for an interesting contrast of textures... fill a tall glass hurricane for a quick centerpiece.

Fall Harvest Party Treats

Squash Fritters

Tamela James
Grove City, OH

In our family, we're fans of yellow squash. My usual recipe for frying squash is just the southern version I grew up making and eating. This recipe is so yummy with any soup, or just as a tasty snack...enjoy!

4 yellow squash, cut into
   large chunks
1 egg, beaten
1/2 c. buttermilk
3/4 c. onion, chopped
3/4 c. all-purpose flour

3/4 t. baking powder
1/8 t. salt
1/4 t. pepper
2 T. shredded Cheddar cheese
2 T. grated Parmesan cheese
oil for frying

Add squash to a saucepan of boiling water. Cook over medium heat until fork-tender; drain, mash and drain again. In a bowl, combine remaining ingredients except oil; mix well. Add squash and mix again. Heat 1/2-inch oil in a saucepan over medium-high heat. Drop squash mixture by medium scoops into hot oil. Cook until golden. Drain on paper towels; serve hot. To reheat any leftover fritters, place on a baking sheet; bake at 350 degrees for 10 minutes. Fritters will crisp up again. Makes about 2-1/2 dozen.

Hollow out a speckled turban squash and fill with a favorite
dip for veggies or chips...a fall twist on a serving bowl!

Greek Island Dip

Sonya Labbe
Quebec, Canada

This is a quick dip with a Greek flair! When I have people over, I love to serve this dip...it's a big hit at parties. I was inspired by a dip that I sampled in Greece, where it is served with cocktails and wine.

1-1/2 c. crumbled feta cheese
1/2 c. toasted cashews
1/2 c. milk
juice of 1/2 lemon
1 t. dried oregano
1/4 t. red pepper flakes
1 t. pepper
1/4 c. green olives, chopped
1/4 c. Kalamata olives, pitted
   and chopped
sliced pita bread or pita chips

In a food processor, combine feta cheese, cashews, milk, lemon juice and seasonings. Process until smooth and creamy. Spoon dip into a serving bowl; garnish with olives. Serve immediately with pita bread or pita chips, or cover and chill until serving time. Serves 8.

Make your game-day celebration easier by preparing your dips and spreads in advance. They're usually fine in the fridge for up to 3 days, and the flavor may be even better!

Fall Harvest
Party Treats

Pumpkin Hummus

Jill Ball
Highland, UT

*This is usually one of the first items to go at any party.
The pumpkin flavor isn't overpowering and it's easy,
quick and yummy...my kind of recipe!*

1 c. canned pumpkin
1 c. black beans, drained
   and rinsed
1/2 c. cannellini beans, drained
   and rinsed

2 T. extra-virgin olive oil
2 cloves garlic, chopped
juice of 2 lemons
1/2 t. ground cumin
salt and pepper to taste

Combine all ingredients in a food processor; process until smooth.
Transfer to a serving bowl and serve, or cover and chill. Makes about
2-1/2 cups.

Pack a tailgating kit for the trunk. Fill a tote bag with paper towels,
wet wipes, trash bags, a bottle opener and matches for the grill...
all those must-haves that are so easy to forget. Now enjoy your
game day, knowing that you're ready for anything!

Fall Cooking
with Family & Friends

Bacon-Wrapped Peppers

Beckie Apple
Grannis, AR

This is one of our favorite treats from the garden! We grow a variety of summer vegetables, including hot banana peppers and jalapeño peppers. They're delicious with any grilled meat or as party snacks.

8 hot banana peppers or
   10 jalapeño peppers
4-oz. block Cheddar cheese,
   cut in strips to fit peppers

8 to 10 mini cocktail sausages
8 to 10 slices bacon

Split peppers down one side; remove seed pod cores. Inside each pepper, place a cheese strip and a sausage. Press peppers closed; wrap each pepper from top to bottom with a bacon slice. Secure at both ends with a wooden toothpick. Line a shallow 13"x9" baking pan with aluminum foil; spray with non-stick vegetable spray. Arrange peppers in pan. Bake, uncovered, at 375 degrees for 25 minutes, or until bacon is crisp. Makes 8 to 10 servings.

Parmesan-Onion Chips

Sheri Kohl
Wentzville, MO

We love sharing these hot snacks while watching football together, or on a chilly evening around the fireplace.

1/2 c. mayonnaise
1/2 c. shredded Parmesan cheese
1/4 c. onion, finely chopped

1 t. milk
1/8 t. garlic powder
1/2 loaf cocktail rye bread

In a bowl, combine all ingredients except rye bread; mix well. Spread mixture on slices of rye bread; arrange on a broiler pan. Broil for a few minutes, until bubbly and golden; serve hot. Makes 6 to 8 servings.

For stand-up parties, make it easy on guests...
serve foods that can be eaten in just one or two bites.

Fall Harvest
Party Treats

Onion Jam & Cream Cheese Spread

Karen Wilson
Defiance, OH

This spread is delicious on crackers, and just a little different.
The onion jam can be made up to three weeks ahead...
it's handy to have on hand for drop-in guests.

1/4 c. oil
1/2 c. sugar
4 c. sweet onions, coarsely
   chopped
1/4 t. salt

1/8 t. pepper
1/2 c. red wine vinegar
8-oz. pkg. cream cheese,
   softened
favorite snack crackers

Heat oil in a large skillet over medium heat. Sprinkle sugar over oil; cook and stir for about 10 minutes, until mixture turns a caramel color. Add onions; season with salt and pepper. Cook over medium heat for 12 minutes, stirring often. Stir in vinegar. Reduce heat to low; simmer for 30 minutes. Remove from heat; cool and transfer to a covered container. Refrigerate up to 3 weeks. To serve, place softened cream cheese on a serving plate. Top with one cup of onion jam. Serve with your favorite crackers. Serves 8.

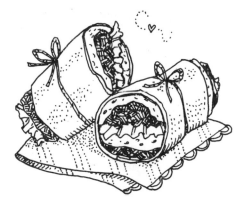

When taking sandwiches to a social, don't just wrap them
in foil...make them really special. Wrap each one in wax paper
and seal with a pretty label to identify what's inside.

Fall Cooking
with *Family & Friends*

Low-Sodium Party Mix

Patricia Wheetman
Elizabethton, TN

I love party mix, but am on sodium restrictions. This version is much lower in sodium than the usual mix, but still has the great flavor and crunch of the all-time holiday favorite! I cut down the seasoning salt by half and doubled the garlic powder from the usual recipe, but you may wish to omit the seasoning salt altogether to reduce the sodium even more.

6 c. bite-size crispy corn cereal squares
6 c. bite-size crispy rice cereal squares
6 c. bite-size crispy wheat cereal squares
6 c. doughnut-shaped oat cereal
2 c. unsalted raw mixed nuts
2 c. unsalted pretzels
1 c. unsalted butter, cut into chunks
1/4 c. low-sodium Worcestershire sauce
2 t. garlic powder
1/2 t. onion powder
Optional: 1 t. seasoning salt

In a roaster pan or other large pan, combine cereals, nuts and pretzels; set aside. Place butter in a microwave-safe 4 to 6-cup glass bowl. Microwave until butter is melted. Stir Worcestershire sauce and seasonings into melted butter until well mixed. Drizzle butter mixture over cereal mixture; stir gently but thoroughly to ensure even coating. Bake, uncovered, at 250 degrees for one hour, stirring every 15 minutes. Cool; store in a large popcorn tin or other covered container. Makes 30 cups.

Fill small paper bags with a favorite snack mix for a tasty trick-or-treat bag, or set out a plastic pumpkin filled with treats for guests to enjoy.

Fall Harvest
Party Treats

Lora's BBQ-Sweet Chili Shredded Chicken

Lora Cotton
Richmond, TX

My husband and I had been invited to a couples baby shower, but knew that odds were against his being able to eat 98% of any foods made available. He suffers from gastroparesis and cannot eat many things. So I tossed this together in the slow cooker...I was absolutely amazed by the final result. Since then, we've enjoyed the chicken in sandwiches, over rice and even as a baked potato topper!

2-1/2 lbs. frozen boneless,
   skinless chicken breasts
onion powder and garlic powder
   to taste
2 c. chicken broth

18-oz. bottle favorite barbecue
   sauce, divided
16-oz. bottle sweet chili sauce
   & marinade, divided
sandwich buns, split

Season frozen chicken with onion and garlic powder; arrange in a 5-quart crockpot. In a bowl, combine chicken broth and 1/2 bottle of barbecue sauce; spoon over chicken. Cover and cook on low setting for 4 to 6 hours, or on high setting for 2 to 3 hours, until chicken is very tender. Drain 75 to 90% of liquid from crock. Using an electric mixer set on low to medium speed, shred chicken in crock. Add remaining barbecue sauce and at least 1/2 bottle of sweet chili sauce, to taste; stir to combine and heat through. Turn slow cooker to low or warm for serving. Serve shredded chicken on buns. Serves 10 to 15.

Mini versions of favorite sandwiches are so appealing
on party platters...fun for sampling too! Simply serve in
a variety of slider buns instead of full-size buns.

Pizza Rolls

Karen Wilson
Defiance, OH

My grandkids love the pizza rolls from a local pizza restaurant, so I decided to turn my soft pretzel recipe into pizza rolls for them. They've become a favorite whenever the grandkids visit. Of course, I have to triple the recipe for them!

1 c. warm water, not over
   105 degrees
2 T. sugar
2 t. instant dry yeast
2 T. oil
1 t. salt

2-1/2 to 3 c. bread flour or
   all-purpose flour
40 pepperoni slices
8 mozzarella sticks
garlic salt to taste
Garnish: warmed pizza sauce

In a bowl, whisk together warm water, sugar and yeast. Let stand for 5 minutes; whisk in oil and salt. Add 2 to 2-1/2 cups flour; stir until flour is thoroughly blended in. Spread remaining flour on a pastry cloth or counter; knead dough until smooth and elastic. Place dough in a bowl; cover with a tea towel and a plastic bag. Let rise for 30 minutes. Punch dough down. On floured surface, roll into a 24-inch by 6-inch rectangle. Cut into 6-inch by 3-inch slices. Top each slice with 5 pepperoni slices (folded in half) and one cheese stick. Roll up and pinch edges to seal. Place rolls seam-side down on a parchment paper-lined baking sheet, 2 inches apart. Bake at 400 degrees for 12 to 13 minutes, until golden. As soon as rolls are removed from oven, spritz with non-stick vegetable spray; sprinkle with garlic salt. Serve with warmed pizza sauce. Serves 4.

A spine-chilling accent for your party punch bowl! Fill a plastic surgical glove with water; tie tightly and freeze. Remove from glove to reveal an icy, ghostly hand.

Fall Harvest
Party Treats

Saucy Party Meatballs

*Gladys Brehm
Quakertown, PA*

*Everyone's favorite meatballs! So easy to make...
great for holiday get-togethers of any kind.*

14-oz. can jellied cranberry sauce
12-oz. bottle chili sauce
1 T. Worcestershire sauce

32-oz. pkg. frozen meatballs,
thawed

Combine all sauces in a 4-quart slow cooker; mix well. Add meatballs;
stir gently to coat with sauce. Cover and cook on high setting for 2 to
4 hours, until bubbly and heated through. Turn slow cooker to low or
warm setting for serving. Makes about 2-1/2 dozen.

Bacon-Wrapped Bread Sticks

*Ann Farris
Biscoe, AR*

*These are easy and everyone always wants more.
You may want to double the recipe!*

24 thin slices bacon
2 11-oz. tubes refrigerated
bread stick dough

1 c. grated Parmesan cheese
2 t. garlic powder

Wrap a slice of bacon around each unbaked bread stick. Arrange on
parchment paper-lined baking sheets. Bake at 375 degrees for 15 to
20 minutes, watching closely, until bread is golden and bacon is crisp.
In a shallow bowl, combine cheese and garlic powder. Roll warm bread
sticks in cheese mixture; serve warm. Makes 2 dozen.

Use fun shapes of cookie cutters to cut cheese slices for
relish plates...autumn leaves, acorns, crescent moons.

Fall Cooking
with *Family & Friends*

Bart's Southwestern Salsa

Garilyn Bardash
Breaux Bridge, LA

This was my husband Bart's salsa recipe. Everywhere we'd bring this dish, it was gone in no time. It's fresh, healthy and delicious all at the same time!

3 avocados, peeled, pitted and cut into chunks
2 to 3 c. ice water
1/4 c. lemon juice
1 c. purple onion, chopped
3 stalks celery, chopped
1 green pepper, finely chopped
8 roma tomatoes, chopped
1/2 c. fresh cilantro or parsley, chopped
1 bunch green onions, chopped
1/4 c. olive oil
3 T. garlic, chopped
1 T. dried basil
1 t. chili powder
Creole seasoning and cayenne pepper to taste

In a large bowl, cover avocado chunks with ice water; add lemon juice and mix gently. Let stand for 20 minutes; drain well and return to bowl. Combine avocados and remaining ingredients; toss to mix well. Cover and chill for about 2 hours. Serves 12 to 15.

We all like to exchange recipes at family get-togethers, so drop a note in the mail ahead of time, asking everyone to jot theirs down. Make plenty of extra copies to share.

Fall Harvest
Party Treats

Bacon-Ranch Veggie Crescent Pizza

Kimberly Redeker
Savoy, IL

This is a delicious twist on a popular party food. Whenever I make it for an event, the dish comes home completely clean! The ranch and bacon make it irresistible, and it's super fun to arrange the veggies in seasonal or event-themed designs.

2 8-oz. tubes refrigerated
   crescent rolls
8-oz. pkg cream cheese, softened
1/2 c. sour cream
1-oz. pkg. ranch salad dressing
   mix

2 c. broccoli, green pepper,
   tomatoes, carrots and/or
   olives, finely chopped
1/2 lb. bacon, crisply cooked
   and chopped

Spread out rolls on an ungreased baking sheet, pressing seams together. Bake at 375 degrees for 9 to 12 minutes, until golden; cool. In a large bowl, mix cream cheese, sour cream and salad dressing mix. Spread mixture over baked crescent rolls; arrange vegetables on top as desired. Sprinkle evenly with bacon. Cut into squares; cover and chill until ready to serve. Makes 15 to 20 servings.

Serving up burgers & dogs from the grill? A muffin tin makes a terrific condiment server. Fill each cup with something different... how about catsup, mustard, pickle relish, hot pepper sauce, horseradish and mayonnaise?

Fall Cooking
with Family & Friends

BBQ Ham Buns

Pam Hepler
Windsor, CO

My grandma made these, my mom made these, I still make them and now my daughter does too...we all love them! I grew up in Pennsylvania eating chipped chopped ham from the deli, which is called for in the original recipe, but delis here in Colorado and Arizona have no idea what that is. So I cut my deli ham into long, thin strips instead. The buns are just as delicious!

1 lb. thin-sliced deli baked ham,
   cut into thin strips
1 T. butter
1/2 c. catsup
1/4 c. vinegar
2 T. water

4 t. brown sugar, packed
1/2 t. mustard
1/8 t. paprika
Optional: cheese slices
4 to 6 hamburger buns, split
   and toasted

In a large saucepan, heat ham with butter over low heat until warmed through. Stir in remaining ingredients except buns and optional cheese. Simmer for 5 to 10 minutes, stirring occasionally, until ham is well coated. If desired, place a slice of cheese on bun before adding ham. Serve ham mixture spooned onto toasted hamburger buns. Makes 4 to 6 sandwiches.

For a new party treat, mix up some tangy ranch pickles! Simply add a packet of ranch seasoning mix to an undrained 24-ounce jar of your favorite pickle spears. Stir gently; add lid and shake well. Chill for 24 hours and serve.

Fall Harvest Party Treats

Reuben Spread

Bobbi Crosson
Toledo, OH

This hearty spread has become a favorite of several of my friends, some of whom never cared for Reuben sandwiches. I've been taking it to events and everyone wants the recipe!

1/4 lb. deli corned beef, chopped into small pieces
8-oz. pkg. low-fat cream cheese, softened
14-1/2 oz. can sauerkraut, drained, rinsed and any larger pieces chopped

2 c. shredded Swiss cheese
3 T. Thousand Island salad dressing
cocktail rye bread or whole-wheat crackers

Combine all ingredients except bread or crackers in a 3-quart slow cooker coated with non-stick vegetable spray. (The spray will prevent burning around the edges.) Cover and cook on high setting for one hour, or until cheeses melt, stirring several times. Turn to low setting for serving. Serve warm on cocktail rye bread or whole-wheat crackers. Makes 12 servings.

Serve up hot & tasty sandwiches at your next tailgating party... right out of a slow cooker! Plug it into a power inverter that draws from your car battery.

Fall Cooking
with *Family & Friends*

Cajun Crab Dip

Denise Webb
Guyton, GA

My hubby and I always loved treating ourselves to this dip from the deli. Now I can make it myself. And mine is better...shhhh! Serve with crisp baguette slices or tortilla chips.

8-oz. pkg. cream cheese,
  softened
1/3 c. sour cream
1 T. hot pepper sauce
1-1/2 t. Worcestershire sauce
1-1/2 t. Cajun seasoning

1/2 t. Italian seasoning
1/2 t. garlic powder
1/2 c. shredded Cheddar cheese
3 green onions, chopped
8-oz. pkg. imitation crabmeat,
  flaked

In a large bowl, combine all ingredients except Cheddar cheese, green onions and crabmeat. With an electric mixer on medium speed, beat ingredients together well. Gently fold in cheese, onions and crabmeat. Cover and refrigerate for at least 2 hours. Makes about 2 cups.

Herbed Vegetable Dip

Theresa Wehmeyer
Rosebud, MO

This dip is always well received at parties and family gatherings. It's quick & easy to prepare too! Serve with assorted fresh cut vegetables.

1 c. mayonnaise
1 c. sour cream
1 T. dried, minced onions
1 T. dried parsley

1 t. dried dill weed
1 t. seasoned salt
1/2 t. garlic powder

Combine all ingredients in a bowl; mix well. For best flavor, cover and refrigerate overnight before serving. Makes about 2 cups.

Going tailgating? Pack a scout-style pocketknife with can opener, corkscrew and other utensils in your picnic kit... so handy!

Fall Harvest
Party Treats

Water Chestnut-Bacon Appetizers

Janis Parr
Ontario, Canada

I got to sample this appetizer at a "potluck for the girls" I attended. The recipe makes quite a bit of sauce, but believe me, not a drop will be wasted! The combination of crunchy water chestnuts wrapped in juicy bacon and covered in this delicious sauce makes eating just one, impossible.

2 8-oz. cans whole water
   chestnuts, drained and rinsed
1 lb. bacon, slices cut into thirds
1 c. catsup

1/2 c. soy sauce
1/2 c. brown sugar, packed
1/4 c. white vinegar

Wrap each water chestnut in a piece of bacon; secure with a wooden toothpick. Arrange in an ungreased 11"x7" baking pan; set aside. In a small bowl, combine remaining ingredients, stirring well. Spoon sauce over chestnuts, covering well; spread any remaining sauce over top. Bake, uncovered, at 400 degrees for 40 to 50 minutes, until sauce is hot and bubbly. Let cool slightly before serving. Serves 8 to 10.

October gave a party;
The leaves by hundreds came.
The chestnuts, oaks and maples,
And leaves of every name.

–George Cooper

Fall Cooking
with Family & Friends

Charlie Brown's Party Punch
Kathleen Strunk
Chandler, AZ

Every year in October as our family grew, we shared a special meal called the Great Pumpkin Feast. We prepared fall-themed foods and always made this delicious punch. We would decorate the table, make crafts together and watch "It's the Great Pumpkin, Charlie Brown." Our memories of these happy celebrations are as sweet as this special beverage.

3-oz. pkg. orange gelatin mix
1-1/2 c. sugar
2 c. boiling water
46-oz. can pineapple juice

1-1/4 c. lemon juice
several scoops vanilla ice cream
32-oz. bottle club soda, chilled

In a bowl, dissolve gelatin mix and sugar in boiling water; set aside. In a large bowl, combine pineapple juice, lemon juice and gelatin mixture; stir well. Cover and chill at least 3 hours. When ready to serve, pour mixture into a punch bowl; add scoops of ice cream. Pour club soda over all; soda will fizz. Serve immediately. Makes about 3 quarts.

A clear glass punch bowl is a must for entertaining family & friends.
Serve up a layered salad, a fruity punch or a sweet dessert trifle...
even fill it with water and floating candles to serve as a centerpiece!

Fall Harvest
Party Treats

Fabulous Fall Snack

Lynnette Jones
East Flat Rock, NC

My family has enjoyed this snack mix for many years. Wrapped up in little bags and tied with a bow, it makes a cute gift, too!

16-oz. jar dry-roasted peanuts
12-oz. pkg. butterscotch chips
12-oz. pkg. white chocolate chips
10-oz. pkg. chocolate-covered
  raisins

1 c. golden raisins
16-oz. pkg. autumn mix mellow
  creme candies
11.4-oz. pkg. candy-coated
  chocolates in seasonal colors

Combine all ingredients in a large bowl or roaster pan; toss to mix well. Store in a covered container. Makes 30 to 40 servings.

When a snack mix recipe makes lots of servings, spoon it into a large bowl or pail and add a scoop. A stack of snack-size paper bags nearby will make it easy for everyone to help themselves...or even take it along for the road!

Fall Cooking
with *Family & Friends*

Sausage & Kraut Sandwiches

Virginia Campbell
Clifton Forge, VA

A perfect savory Oktoberfest meal on a bun! So satisfying and filling. The scent of the dish cooking is irresistible aromatherapy. Use any kind of hard roll you like...white, wheat, pumpernickel and marble rye are all scrumptious. I like to set out a variety of yummy mustards, like spicy brown mustard, stone-ground mustard, Dijon mustard, hot mustard or honey mustard.

1-1/2 to 2 lbs. smoked pork
   sausage, cut into bite-size
   pieces
27-oz. can sauerkraut
1 c. apple cider or juice
4 tart apples, peeled, cored
   and chopped

1/4 c. onion, chopped
1/4 c. brown sugar, packed
1 t. caraway seed
4 to 6 hard rolls, split and
   warmed, if desired
Garnish: favorite mustards

Place smoked sausage in a 4-quart slow cooker; set aside. In a large bowl, combine undrained sauerkraut, apple cider or juice, apples, onion, brown sugar and caraway seed; spoon over sausage. Cover and cook on low setting for 4 to 5 hours, stirring occasionally, until hot and bubbly. Spoon sausage mixture into rolls; serve with a choice of mustards on the side. Makes 4 to 6 sandwiches.

No spills, no mess! Set a muffin tin inside a small carry-all basket.
Add your filled beverage glasses and carry with confidence.

Fall Harvest
Party Treats

Favorite Wassail

Vicky Lamb
Grantsville, UT

Enjoy the taste of the holidays! I've been making this for more than 40 years. I start serving it on Thanksgiving Day and don't stop until New Year's Day has ended, keeping it special for the holidays. My kids and grandkids know the holiday season is officially here when they walk into my house and smell this heating on the stove or in the slow cooker. It not only tastes great, but makes the house smell wonderful.

1 gal. apple juice	2 t. whole allspice
1 qt. cranberry juice cocktail	1 t. whole cloves
2 t. aromatic bitters	1 large orange, unpeeled

Combine juices, bitters and allspice in a large stockpot or slow cooker. Press cloves into orange; add to juice mixture. Cover and cook on low setting for one to 2 hours, to blend flavors. Cool to room temperature. Strain; store in emptied juice bottles or in a large pitcher. Put lids on and store in refrigerator. Reheat as needed. Makes 20 servings.

Grandma's Autumn Tea

Gladys Kielar
Whitehouse, OH

Fruit juices combine with pumpkin pie spice to make a delicious fall tea. Great warm or cold!

5 tea bags	1/3 c. lemon juice
5 c. boiling water	1/2 c. sugar
5 c. unsweetened apple juice	1/4 t. pumpkin pie spice
2 c. cranberry juice cocktail	

Place tea bags in a large heat-proof pitcher; add boiling water. Cover and steep for 8 minutes; discard tea bags. Add remaining ingredients; stir until sugar is dissolved. Serve warm or chilled. Makes 3 quarts.

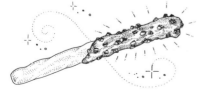

For an easy themed party treat, dip pretzel rods in melted candy melts and roll them in colorful sprinkles.

Fall Cooking
with *Family & Friends*

BLT Stuffed Eggs

Mel Chencharick
Julian, PA

*I'm always looking for a new way to serve deviled eggs. This recipe
is simple, yet gives the eggs a great taste. Take these to
a picnic or party and watch how fast they go!*

6 eggs, hard-boiled, peeled and
  halved lengthwise
1/4 c. mayonnaise
5 slices bacon, crisply cooked,
  crumbled and divided

2 to 3 cherry tomatoes, finely
  chopped
1 T. dried parsley
salt and pepper to taste
Optional: shredded lettuce

Remove egg yolks to a small bowl; set aside egg whites. Mash yolks;
stir in mayonnaise, 2/3 of bacon, tomatoes and parsley until well
blended. Season with salt and pepper. Fill egg whites evenly with yolk
mixture; top with remaining bacon. Cover and refrigerate for one hour
before serving. If desired, arrange on a platter covered with shredded
lettuce. Makes one dozen.

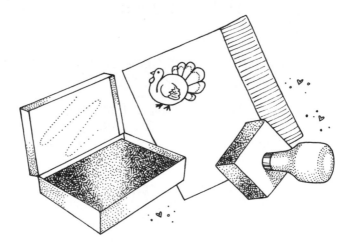

Yummy finger foods call for lots of paper napkins. Dress up
plain napkins in a jiffy with a large turkey rubber stamp and
a colorful stamp pad...so festive!

Fall Harvest Party Treats

Copycat Spinach Dip

Hannah McCoy
Arbuckle, CA

This is a copycat recipe from a favorite Italian restaurant. It's always a hit at potlucks! Serve with slices of toasted baguette.

1/4 c. grated Parmesan cheese
1/4 c. grated Romano cheese
1/4 c. mayonnaise
1 clove garlic, finely minced
1/2 t. dried basil
1/4 t. garlic salt
salt and pepper to taste

14-oz. can artichoke hearts,
  drained and chopped
1/2 c. frozen chopped spinach,
  thawed and drained
1/4 c. shredded mozzarella
  cheese

In a large bowl, blend together Parmesan and Romano cheeses, mayonnaise, garlic and seasonings. Add artichokes and spinach; mix until blended. Spray a 9" pie plate with non-stick vegetable spray; spoon in dip and top with mozzarella cheese. Bake, uncovered, at 350 degrees for 25 minutes, or until hot and bubbly. Serves 4 to 6.

Pack disposable plates and cups for a game day get-together.
Who wants to do the dishes after having so much fun?

Fall Cooking
with *Family & Friends*

Shrimp Cheese Spread

Leona Krivda
Belle Vernon, PA

This is a very easy recipe that you can put together at the last minute to impress your guests. I've been making it for so long, I'm not sure where I got the recipe. Always a big hit at parties!

2 8-oz. pkgs. cream cheese,
   softened
1-1/2 t. lemon juice
12-oz. pkg. frozen cooked salad
   shrimp, thawed and drained

1 c. catsup
1/4 c. chili sauce
1 T. horseradish sauce
snack crackers

In a large bowl, blend cream cheese and lemon juice. Add shrimp; mix well and form into a ball. Place on a serving plate; set aside. In another bowl, mix remaining ingredients except crackers; spoon over the shrimp ball. Serve with crackers. Serves 8 to 10.

Spoon dips and spreads into pretty crocks or vintage canning jars... they're ideal as hostess gifts. Add a box of crisp crackers and tie on a spreader with a pretty ribbon...sure to be appreciated!

Fall Harvest **Party Treats**

Apple-Cranberry Hot Cider

Terry Kenaston
Keizer, OR

I first made this recipe in 1980, and it instantly became a family favorite. I made it every Halloween before taking my three little boys trick-or-treating. They are grown now, but we all still enjoy this wonderful hot cider.

64-oz. bottle apple cider	1/4 c. brown sugar, packed
48-oz. bottle cranberry juice	4 4-inch cinnamon sticks
cocktail	1-1/2 t. whole cloves

Stir all ingredients together in a large pot. If desired, enclose whole spices in a spice bag before adding. Bring to a boil over medium-high heat. Reduce heat to low; simmer for 20 minutes, stirring occasionally. Makes 3-1/2 quarts.

Autumn is the perfect time of year to hit all the best craft shows, flea markets and tag sales. Call your best girlfriends, pack a basket of snacks and a thermos of spiced cider, and head out for a day of shopping fun.

Fall Cooking
with Family & Friends

Balsamic Candied Walnuts

Angela Murphy
Tempe, AZ

For party nibbling or quick gifts, you can't go wrong
with these sweet and peppery nuts.

2 T. canola oil
2 T. balsamic vinegar
1/8 t. pepper

2 c. walnut halves
1/2 c. brown sugar, packed

In a heavy skillet over medium heat, combine oil, vinegar and pepper. Cook and stir until well blended. Add walnuts; cook for about 4 minutes, until toasted. Sprinkle with brown sugar. Cook and stir for 2 to 4 minutes, until brown sugar dissolves. Spread on aluminum foil to cool. Store in an airtight container. Makes 2 cups.

Ranch Snacking Seeds

Cathy Hillier
Salt Lake City, UT

Now that they're older, my kids say this is the best part
of carving a Jack-o'-Lantern!

1/4 c. oil
3 c. fresh pumpkin seeds, rinsed
and drained

1/4 to 1/3 c. ranch salad dressing
mix

Heat oil in a large skillet over medium heat. Add pumpkin seeds and sauté for 5 minutes, or until lightly golden. Using a slotted spoon, transfer seeds to an ungreased 15"x10" jelly-roll pan. Sprinkle with dressing mix; stir to coat and spread in a single layer. Bake at 325 degrees for 10 to 15 minutes, until crisp. Cool; store in an airtight container for up to 3 weeks. Makes 3 cups.

For a clever porch display, carve your house number into a pumpkin. Set it on the front steps and tuck a lighted votive candle inside.

Fall Harvest
Party Treats

Rosemary Almonds

Kathy Parks
Saint Charles, MO

Great for snacking or gift-giving. I make these during the holidays for family & friends.

2 c. whole almonds
3 T. olive oil
1/2 to 1 t. kosher salt

1/8 to 1/2 t. cayenne pepper
1 T. fresh rosemary,
  finely minced

Spread almonds on an aluminum foil-lined baking sheet; set aside. In a small bowl, mix together remaining ingredients; drizzle over almonds and toss to coat. Bake at 350 degrees for 10 to 15 minutes, stirring once or twice, until evenly golden. Cool; store in an airtight container. Makes 2 cups.

Sugar-Coated Pecans

Trudy Satterwhite
San Antonio, TX

These sweet pecans are so good, it is impossible to stop munching on them! I make several batches of these for the holidays.

1 T. egg white
2 c. pecan halves

1/4 c. sugar
2 t. cinnamon

In a large bowl, beat egg white until foamy. Add pecans and toss until well coated. Combine sugar and cinnamon in a cup; sprinkle over pecans and toss to coat. Spread in a single layer on an ungreased baking sheet. Bake at 300 degrees for 30 minutes, or until golden. Cool on wax paper; store in an airtight container. Makes about 2 cups.

Stir up some Grizzly Gorp for snacking. Just toss together
two cups bear-shaped graham crackers, one cup mini marshmallows,
one cup peanuts and 1/2 cup raisins. Yum!

Fall Cooking
with *Family & Friends*

Italian Combo Salad

Mariann Raftery
New Rochelle, NY

In my area, there's a deli sandwich called an "Italian Wedge" that's very popular. My own Italian Combo Salad was created with all the ingredients I like on a sandwich, but with pasta instead of the bread. Enjoy!

16-oz. pkg. rotini pasta, uncooked
6-oz. jar marinated artichoke quarters, drained
1/2 c. roasted red peppers, sliced
1 to 2 tomatoes, chopped
1/4 red onion, thinly sliced
1/4 to 1/2 lb. Genova salami, cubed

1/2 round fresh mozzarella cheese, cubed
1 head butter lettuce, cut up
1 head red leaf lettuce, cut up
1/4 c. Italian salad dressing
1/4 c. olive oil
salt and pepper to taste

Cook pasta according to package directions, just until tender. Drain; rinse in cold water and let cool. In a large bowl, combine chopped and sliced vegetables, salami, cheese and lettuces; add cooled pasta. Add remaining ingredients; toss to coat well. Season with additional salt and pepper or salad dressing as desired. Serve immediately, or cover and refrigerate until serving time. Serves 10.

Younger guests will feel so grown up when served bubbly sparkling cider or ginger ale in long-stemmed plastic glasses.

Favorite
Desserts
for Sharing

Fall Cooking
with Family & Friends

Pumpkin Sheet Cake

Charlotte Smith
Tyrone, PA

For serving lots of people, a sheet cake can't be beat! Dress it up for parties...press a candy pumpkin or a piece of candy corn onto each square of cake.

1-1/2 c. sugar
15-oz. can pumpkin
1 c. oil
4 eggs, beaten
2 c. all-purpose flour

2 t. baking powder
1 t. baking soda
1 t. salt
2 t. cinnamon
1/2 t. pumpkin pie spice

Combine all ingredients in a large bowl. Beat with an electric mixer on medium speed for 2 minutes, or until smooth. Pour batter into a greased 15"x10" jelly-roll pan. Bake at 350 degrees for 20 to 25 minutes, until a toothpick inserted in the center tests clean. Cool; frost with Cream Cheese Frosting. Cut into squares. Makes 24 servings.

Cream Cheese Frosting

8-oz. pkg. cream cheese,
    softened
1/2 c. butter, softened

2 t. vanilla extract
4-1/2 c. powdered sugar
Optional: few drops milk

Combine all ingredients except milk in a large bowl. Beat with an electric mixer on medium speed to a spreading consistency. If too thick, add a few drops of milk.

Invite friends over for "just desserts!" Offer 2 to 3 simple homebaked desserts like cobblers, dump cake and fruit pie, ice cream for topping and a steamy pot of coffee...so welcoming!

Favorite Desserts for Sharing

Sweet Pear Cake

Vickie
Gooseberry Patch

This is a lovely, sweet cake that really pleases guests.
Garnish it simply, with powdered sugar and candied nuts.

4 soft ripe pears, peeled, cored
   and thinly sliced
1 c. brown sugar, packed
1 c. sugar
1 c. chopped pecans
3 c. all-purpose flour

2 t. baking soda
1/2 t. salt
1 c. oil
2 eggs, beaten
1 t. vanilla extract

In a large bowl, combine pears, sugars and pecans; toss to mix well and let stand for one hour. Process pear mixture in a blender until puréed; return to bowl and set aside. In another bowl, mix together flour, baking soda and salt. Add flour mixture to pear mixture; stir just until blended. Add oil, eggs and vanilla; mix well. Pour batter into a greased and floured 13"x9" baking pan. Bake at 350 degrees for one hour and 15 minutes. Cool; cut into squares. Serves 12 to 15.

The holidays are just around the corner...time to check the spice rack! Crush a pinch of each spice. If it has a fresh, zingy scent, it's still good. Toss out old-smelling spices and stock up on any that you've used up during the year.

Fall Cooking
with Family & Friends

Jamie's Favorite Cookies

Elisha Nelson
Brookline, MO

These are my husband's absolute favorite cookies! He loves oatmeal and these cookies are the perfect blend of chewy oatmeal and delicious chocolate. I often bake half of the dough and freeze the rest, so I can have freshly baked cookies in minutes for guests. However, I have to hide the dough in the back of the freezer, because my husband loves to sneak them even when they're frozen! Enjoy with a tall glass of milk.

1/2 c. butter, room temperature
3/4 c. brown sugar, packed
1/2 c. sugar
1 extra-large egg, beaten
1 t. vanilla extract
1 c. all-purpose flour

2 c. rolled oats, uncooked
1/2 t. baking powder
1/2 t. baking soda
1/4 t. salt
1/2 to 3/4 c. semi-sweet
   chocolate chips

In a large bowl, beat together butter and sugars. Add egg and vanilla; beat until smooth. Add flour, oats, baking powder, baking soda and salt; mix just until all ingredients are well blended. Fold in chocolate chips. If time allows, cover and chill dough for one hour for best texture. (Cookies will still be delicious without chilling!) Drop dough by walnut-size balls onto greased baking sheets. Bake at 350 degrees for about 9 minutes. Cool on a wire rack. Makes 2 to 3 dozen.

A fun way to serve cake pops or doughnut holes! Simply drill holes in the top of a pumpkin and insert the treat sticks.

Favorite Desserts for Sharing

After-School Date Bars

Lynda Hart
Bluffdale, UT

My mom belonged to a neighborhood group of ladies who played Yahtzee every Thursday. When it was Mom's turn to host, she often made these date bars. Whenever I got home from school on Yahtzee day, there were always leftover bars for Dad and me to share.

1 lb. chopped dates
1/2 c. brown sugar, packed

1 c. water
1 T. all-purpose flour

Mix together all ingredients in a saucepan. Cook over medium heat until thickened, stirring often; set aside. Press slightly more than half of Crust mixture into a greased 13"x9" baking pan. Spread date mixture over crust; sprinkle with remaining crust mixture. Bake at 325 degrees for 20 minutes. Let stand for a few minutes; cut into bars. Make 16 bars.

Crust:

1-1/2 c. all-purpose flour
1-1/2 t. baking soda
2 c. rolled oats, uncooked

1-1/2 c. sugar
3/4 c. butter, melted

Sift together flour and baking soda. Mix in oats and sugar; add melted butter and stir.

For parties and bake sales, bar cookies are just about the easiest dessert to make and serve...and they come in so many tasty varieties!

Fall Cooking
with *Family & Friends*

Autumn Apple-Pear Pie

Rachel Boyd
Defiance, OH

I had some pears and apples getting rather ripe, so I decided to make this pie. It was an instant hit with everyone! Top with spiced whipped cream for extra goodness.

9-inch pie crust, unbaked
1/2 t. cardamom
4 apples, peeled, cored and
  chopped
4 to 6 pears, peeled, cored
  and chopped
1 c. fresh cranberries
1/2 c. sugar

1/2 t. cinnamon
1/2 t. dark corn syrup
1/2 c. plus 2 t. brown sugar,
  packed
1/2 c. chopped pecans
1/3 c. rolled oats, uncooked
1/2 c. chilled butter, divided

Arrange pie crust in a 9" pie plate; sprinkle with cardamom and set aside. In a large bowl, combine fruits, sugar, cinnamon and corn syrup. Toss to mix well; spoon into pie crust. In a separate bowl, combine brown sugar, pecans, oats and 6 tablespoons butter; mix with a fork until crumbly. Spoon brown sugar mixture over fruit mixture; dot with remaining butter. Bake at 350 degrees for at least 45 minutes, until golden. Cut into wedges; serve warm. Serves 8.

Celebrate Johnny Appleseed's birthday on September 26th...
a terrific reason to enjoy a tasty apple dessert.

Favorite Desserts for **Sharing**

Deluxe Apple Crunch

Susan Wilson
Johnson City, TN

This is a very rich and tasty apple dessert...especially good in the fall with a hot cup of coffee.

6 apples, cored, peeled and
   sliced, or 2 21-oz. cans
   apple pie filling
1/2 c. sugar
nutmeg or cinnamon to taste
1 c. brown sugar, packed
1/2 c. butter

1/2 c. all-purpose flour
1/2 c. rolled oats, uncooked
3/4 c. chopped pecans
1/2 c. raisins
Garnish: whipped cream,
   ice cream or sliced Cheddar
   cheese

Spread apples or pie filling in a buttered 9"x9" baking pan. Sprinkle with sugar and nutmeg or cinnamon; set aside. In a bowl, blend remaining ingredients except garnish until mixture resembles coarse meal. Spread over apples. Bake at 325 degrees for one hour. Serve warm, topped with whipped cream, ice cream or a slice of Cheddar cheese. Makes 8 servings.

Serve ice cream-topped desserts to a party crowd,
the quick & easy way! Scoop ice cream ahead of time
and freeze in paper muffin liners.

Fall Cooking
with *Family & Friends*

Cranberry-Walnut Oatmeal Cookies

Karen McCann
Marion, OH

This is a versatile recipe. For variety, I have added golden raisins or chopped dates. I like to use a large cookie scoop, which makes two dozen cookies, and I bake them about 5 minutes longer.

3/4 c. butter-flavored shortening
3/4 c. brown sugar, packed
1/2 c. sugar
2 eggs, beaten
2 t. vanilla extract
1 c. all-purpose flour

1 t. baking soda
1/4 t. salt
3 c. old-fashioned oats, uncooked
1-1/2 c. dried cranberries
1 c. chopped walnuts

With an electric mixer on medium speed, beat shortening and sugars in a large bowl until blended. Beat in eggs and vanilla; set aside. In a small bowl, combine flour, baking soda and salt. Add to shortening mixture and beat until smooth. Stir in oats, cranberries and walnuts. Cover and refrigerate until chilled. Drop dough by rounded tablespoonfuls onto parchment paper-lined baking sheets, about 2 inches apart. Flatten cookies to one inch. Bake at 325 degrees for 10 to 12 minutes, until golden; cool on baking sheets for 2 minutes. Remove cookies to a wire rack and cool completely. Makes 3 dozen.

Need a quick gift? Tuck a variety of wrapped cookies inside a plastic pumpkin pail. Remember to include copies of the recipes. All treats, no tricks!

Favorite Desserts for Sharing

Salted Caramel Pretzel Brownies

*Mandy Ryeczek
Uniontown, PA*

I've made this delicious dessert several times for the ladies at the personal-care home where I work. Every time, they have loved it and always asked for a second helping! I couldn't be more happy to share this sweet, easy recipe with you all. Enjoy these bite-size yummy sweet and salty delights!

18.3-oz. pkg. fudge brownie mix
2 eggs, beaten
1/4 c. water
2/3 c. oil
3 c. pretzel twists
12-oz. jar caramel topping
coarse sea salt to taste

Prepare brownie mix with eggs, water and oil according to package instructions. Pour 1/3 of batter into a parchment paper-lined 13"x9" baking pan; spread to coat bottom of pan evenly. Add pretzels in 2 even layers over batter, covering the entire surface. Carefully spoon remaining batter over pretzels. Bake at 350 degrees for 30 minutes, or until a toothpick inserted in the center tests clean. Set pan on a wire rack to cool. Spoon caramel topping evenly over brownies. (If topping is too thick, spoon it into a small bowl and microwave for 30 seconds to thin.) Sprinkle with salt; cool completely. Lift brownies out of pan by parchment paper "handles" and cut into bars. Serve warm, or cool to room temperature. Makes 12 to 15 brownies.

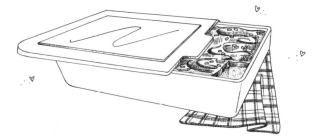

If you see a vintage cake pan with its own slide-on lid at a tag sale, snap it up! It's indispensable for toting cakes and bar cookies to picnics and potlucks.

Fall Cooking
with *Family & Friends*

Milk Chocolate Brownies

Carolyn Gochenaur
Howe, IN

*My sister-in-law gave me this recipe and it's been
a favorite for many years.*

1/2 c. butter, melted
2 c. plus 2 T. sugar, divided
4 eggs, beaten
2 t. vanilla extract
1-1/2 c. all-purpose flour

1/2 c. baking cocoa
1/2 t. salt
1 c. flaked coconut
1/2 c. milk chocolate chips
1/2 c. chopped pecans

In a large bowl, mix together melted butter and 2 cups sugar. Add eggs
and vanilla; stir until well mixed and set aside. In another bowl, sift
together flour, baking cocoa and salt; add to butter mixture and stir well.
Add coconut and stir until just mixed. Pour batter into a greased and
floured 13"x9" baking pan; sprinkle with chocolate chips, pecans and
remaining sugar. Bake at 350 degrees for 25 minutes, or until a
toothpick comes out clean. Cool; cut into squares. Makes 15 brownies.

Turn a tried & true cake recipe into yummy cupcakes...so pretty
to serve, such fun to eat! Fill greased muffin cups 2/3 full of
cake batter. Bake at 350 degrees until a toothpick tests clean,
about 18 to 20 minutes. Cool and frost.

Favorite Desserts for Sharing

Trick-or-Treat Cookie Bars

Nola Coons
Gooseberry Patch

Perfect for using up the last of the Halloween candy! You can use just about any kind of chocolate candy...we even toss in leftover candy-coated chocolates.

2-1/4 c. all-purpose flour	3/4 c. sugar
1/2 t. baking soda	1 t. vanilla extract
1/2 t. salt	2 eggs, room temperature
3/4 c. butter, softened	2 c. chocolate candy bars and/or
1/4 c. light brown sugar, packed	peanut butter cups, chopped

In a large bowl, whisk together flour, baking soda and salt; set aside. In a separate bowl, with an electric mixer on medium speed, beat together butter, sugars and vanilla until fluffy. Beat in eggs, one at a time. Gradually stir flour mixture into butter mixture. Fold in chopped candy. Spray a 9"x9" baking pan with non-stick vegetable spray; line pan with parchment paper, creating "handles" on 2 sides. Coat paper with non-stick vegetable spray; spread batter in pan. Bake at 350 degrees for 40 minutes, or until golden and a toothpick tests clean. Let cool; remove from pan by the "handles" and place on a cutting board. Cut into bars. Makes 16 bars.

Serve up a Bucket o' Bones at your next Halloween party!
Press a mini marshmallow onto each end of a pretzel stick
and dip in melted white chocolate.

Fall Cooking
with Family & Friends

Family Tradition Iced Pumpkin Cookies

Sandy Churchill
West Bridgewater, MA

The basis of this sweet recipe was given to me as a wedding present, and I have tweaked it over the years as a family favorite. My husband and children still rank it their favorite part of Thanksgiving and we often make the cookies together as the start to our holiday mode. Enjoy a new family tradition!

1/2 c. shortening
1 c. sugar
2 eggs, beaten
1 c. canned pumpkin
2 c. all-purpose flour
1 t. baking powder
1 t. salt

2-1/2 t. cinnamon
1/2 t. nutmeg
1/4 t. ground ginger
3/4 c. raisins
3/4 c. dried cranberries
1-1/2 c. chopped pecans

In a large bowl, blend together shortening and sugar. Add remaining ingredients; beat with an electric mixer or stir by hand until well mixed. Drop dough by heaping tablespoonfuls onto greased baking sheets. Bake at 350 degrees for about 15 minutes, until firm to the touch. Cool about 20 minutes. Spread cookies with Icing. Let set for several hours, or overnight if possible. Makes 3 dozen.

Icing:

1 c. powdered sugar
1 t. lemon zest

1 t. lemon juice

Mix together all ingredients until consistency resembles pudding. Add more powdered sugar or lemon juice, as needed.

When the temperature is dropping, treat yourself to a cup of warm mulled cider. Heat a mug of cider to boiling, add an orange spice tea bag and let stand several minutes.

Favorite Desserts
for **Sharing**

White Chocolate
Candy Corn Cookies

Tina Butler
Royse City, TX

On a whim, I pulled out my favorite cake mix cookie recipe and added some cream cheese, white chocolate chips and festive candy corn-colored chocolates. The end result was these Halloween-inspired cookies. During the holidays, I can never keep enough of these in the cookie jar!

3-oz. pkg. cream cheese,
   softened
1/2 c. butter, melted
1 egg, beaten
1 t. vanilla extract

18-1/2 oz. pkg. white or
   yellow cake mix, divided
3/4 c. white chocolate chips
1 c. white chocolate candy corn
   candy-coated chocolates

In a large bowl, combine cream cheese, butter, egg and vanilla. Beat together thoroughly with an electric mixer on medium speed. Add dry cake mix, 1/2 package at a time; beat until well combined. Batter will be thick. Stir in chocolate chips and candies by hand. Cover and refrigerate dough for 30 minutes. Roll dough into one-inch balls; place on parchment paper-lined or ungreased baking sheets, 2 inches apart. Bake at 350 degrees for 10 minutes, or just until set and lightly golden on the bottom (do not allow to brown). Cool on a wire rack. Makes 2 dozen.

Mix up some frosting for Halloween cut-out cookies. For orange pumpkins, add 6 drops yellow and 2 drops red food coloring to a small bowl of white frosting. For black bats, cats and witches' hats, add 2 to 3 drops blue food coloring to a small bowl of dark chocolate frosting. Add some candy sprinkles and have fun decorating!

Fall Cooking
with *Family & Friends*

Sweet Potato Pecan Pie

Christine Fenner
Prescott Valley, AZ

*Sure to be a hit at your next Thanksgiving dinner! You can
substitute puréed pumpkin in place of the sweet potatoes,
if you like. Sometimes I make mini pies with this recipe.*

9-inch pie crust, unbaked
1-1/4 c. sugar
1/2 t. cinnamon
1/2 t. nutmeg
2 eggs
12-oz. can evaporated milk

1 t. vanilla extract
1-1/2 c. cooked sweet potatoes,
   mashed
Garnish: whipped topping or
   ice cream

Arrange pie crust in a 9" pie plate; set aside. In a bowl, blend sugar and
spices. Beat eggs in a separate large bowl; whisk in milk and vanilla.
Add sugar mixture to egg mixture; mix well. Stir in sweet potatoes; beat
until smooth. Pour into pie crust. Bake at 425 degrees for 15 minutes.
Reduce heat to 350 degrees; bake an additional 30 minutes. Remove
from oven; sprinkle with Topping. Return to oven for 10 to 15 minutes,
until topping is golden. Cool on a wire rack. Cut into wedges; serve with
whipped topping or ice cream. Keep refrigerated. Makes 6 to 8 servings.

Topping:

1/3 c. butter
1/3 c. all-purpose flour
1/2 c. brown sugar, packed

1/2 c. flaked coconut
1/2 c. chopped pecans

Combine all ingredients; mix well until crumbly.

For a crisp, golden finish, bake up
your favorite pies in Grandma's
cast-iron skillet.

Favorite Desserts for **Sharing**

Dawn's Doughnut Bread Pudding

Dawn Smith
Cape Girardeau, MO

One day at work, we had an overabundance of doughnuts left over from an event and I hated to throw them away. So I made bread pudding from them...it was a hit! Now, whenever we have leftover doughnuts, they are given to me to make this scrumptious treat. Recipe can easily be halved or doubled depending on how many doughnuts you have. So yummy!

1 doz. doughnuts of any kind,
   cut into quarters or large
   chunks
3 eggs, beaten
1-1/2 c. milk

1 T. vanilla extract
1-1/2 t. cinnamon
Optional: 1 c. raisins,
   1/4 t. nutmeg
1/4 c. butter, melted

In a large bowl, combine all ingredients except melted butter. Stir very gently, as doughnut texture is soft and you want it left in chunks. Spoon into a greased 8"x8" baking pan; drizzle with melted butter. Bake at 350 degrees for 35 to 40 minutes, until a knife tip inserted in the center comes out clean. Make Vanilla Sauce during the last 15 minutes of baking. Serve bread pudding in individual dishes, drizzled with sauce. If serving a large crowd or potluck, bread pudding and sauce may be served separately, for guests to serve themselves. Makes 6 servings.

Vanilla Sauce:

4.6-oz. pkg. cook & serve
   vanilla pudding mix

3 c. milk
1/2 t. vanilla extract

In a saucepan, combine all ingredients over medium heat. Cook, stirring constantly, until thickened yet still runny. Remove from heat.

Press whole cloves into the surface of a pillar candle to form a pattern...just right for a dessert buffet.

Fall Cooking
with Family & Friends

Rocky Road Cookie Bars

Courtney Stultz
Weir, KS

Usually our family tries to eat really healthy, but sometimes we need a "cheat" day. These little bars make a delicious treat. They are fun to make together as a family!

1/2 c. shortening or butter
3/4 c. brown sugar, packed
1/2 t. vanilla extract
1 egg, beaten
1-1/4 c. all-purpose flour
1 t. baking soda

1/2 t. sea salt
1-1/2 c. semi-sweet chocolate
  chips, divided
1/2 c. chopped walnuts
1/2 to 1 c. mini marshmallows

In a bowl, blend together shortening or butter, brown sugar and vanilla until smooth; stir in egg. Add flour, baking soda and salt; mix until dough forms. Fold in one cup chocolate chips. Spread dough evenly in a greased 9"x9" baking pan. Top with walnuts, marshmallows and remaining chocolate chips. Bake at 400 degrees for about 20 minutes, until done in the center and edges start to turn golden. Let cool about 10 minutes; cut into bars. Makes one dozen.

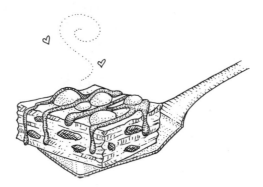

For dazzling bar cookies, melt 1/2 cup chocolate chips with a teaspoon of shortening. Drizzle over uncut cookies. Sprinkle with chopped nuts, seasonal sprinkles or sugar crystals for an extra-special finish. No one will believe they didn't come from a bakery!

Favorite Desserts
for Sharing

Buckeye Brownies

Stephanie Dardani-D'Esposito
Ravena, NY

These are just delicious! This is a great way
to make a boxed brownie special.

18.3-oz. pkg. fudge brownie mix
1/2 c. creamy peanut butter
1/4 c. butter

1 c. powdered sugar
1/8 t. vanilla extract

Prepare brownie mix according to package directions. Spread batter in a 9"x9" baking pan sprayed with non-stick vegetable spray; set aside. In a microwave-safe bowl, combine peanut butter and butter. Microwave until butter melts; mix well. Stir in powdered sugar and vanilla. Roll peanut butter mixture into one-inch balls; arrange over batter. Bake at 350 degrees for 36 to 38 minutes. Cool; cut into squares. Makes 10 brownies.

Cake Mix "Whatever" Cookies

Ron Sheaffer
Austin, TX

Need some cookies right now for drop-in guests, or a last-minute
bake sale notice? This recipe is very adaptable to whatever
you have on hand in the cupboard.

15-1/4 oz. pkg. favorite-flavor
   super-moist cake mix with
   pudding
1/2 c. oil

2 eggs, beaten
1-1/2 c. chocolate chips, chopped
   nuts or rolled oats

Combine all ingredients in a large bowl; mix just until moistened. Drop batter by teaspoonfuls onto baking sheets coated with non-vegetable stick spray. Bake at 350 degrees for 8 to 10 minutes. Makes 3 dozen.

To me there's nothing prettier
Than a well-filled cookie jar!
–Elsie Duncan Yale

Fall Cooking
with *Family & Friends*

Pumpkin Crisp

Bootsie Dominick
Suches, GA

*My husband loves this dessert. It's great to serve at
Thanksgiving or anytime in the fall. Serve topped with
cinnamon or vanilla ice cream...yum!*

18-1/4 oz. pkg. yellow cake
  mix, divided
3/4 c. butter, melted and divided
4 eggs, divided
29-oz. can pumpkin

1/2 c. brown sugar, packed
2/3 c. evaporated milk
2 t. pumpkin pie spice
1/2 c. sugar
1/4 c. chopped nuts

Reserve one cup dry cake mix for topping. In a large bowl, combine
remaining cake mix, 1/2 cup melted butter and one beaten egg. Press
batter into the bottom of a greased 13"x9" baking pan; set aside. In
another bowl, whisk together pumpkin, remaining beaten eggs, brown
sugar, evaporated milk and spice. Spoon over batter in pan. In another
bowl, combine reserved cake mix, remaining melted butter, sugar and
nuts; sprinkle over pumpkin layer in pan. Bake at 350 degrees for
50 minutes. Serve warm or chilled. Makes 8 to 10 servings.

Top off your favorite pumpkin dessert with cinnamon-spice whipped
cream. In a chilled mixing bowl, with an electric mixer on high speed,
beat 2 cups whipping cream, one teaspoon orange extract and
1/4 teaspoon cinnamon until stiff peaks form.

Favorite Desserts for **Sharing**

Apple-Cranberry Crumble

JoAnn
Gooseberry Patch

Scrumptious...and so much easier to make than a pie!

4 c. apples, peeled, cored
   and sliced
1 c. whole-berry cranberry sauce,
   drained if very juicy
1 c. all-purpose flour

1 c. brown sugar, packed
1/4 t. cinnamon
1/3 c. butter, softened
Optional: whipped cream

Arrange apple slices in a greased 8"x8" baking pan. Spoon cranberry sauce over apples; set aside. In a bowl, combine flour, brown sugar, cinnamon and butter; mix with a fork until crumbly and sprinkle over mixture in pan. Bake at 350 degrees for 45 minutes, or until apples are fork-tender and topping is golden. Serve warm or chilled; top with whipped cream, if desired. Serves 6.

Be sure to pick up a pint or two of ice cream in peppermint, cinnamon and other delicious seasonal flavors when they're available. What a special touch for holiday desserts!

Pecan Praline Coffee Cake

Bethi Hendrickson
Danville, PA

This is the best coffee cake ever...so yummy! Great to serve warm with ice cream, or cooled to feed a bunch of hungry teachers.

3 egg whites
3 c. all-purpose flour
4 t. baking powder
1 t. salt

3/4 c. butter, softened
2 c. sugar
1-1/4 c. milk

In a deep bowl, beat egg whites with an electric mixer on high speed until stiff peaks form; set aside. In another bowl, sift together flour, baking powder and salt; set aside. In a third bowl, beat butter and sugar until fluffy. Add flour mixture to butter mixture alternately with milk until combined; do not overmix. Fold in egg whites, using a spoon or spatula. Spread batter in a greased 13"x9" baking pan with high edges (this cake bakes very high). Spread Pecan Topping over batter. Bake at 350 degrees for 40 to 45 minutes, until a toothpick comes out clean. Cut into squares. Serves 12 to 15.

Pecan Topping:

1-1/2 c. chopped pecans
3/4 c. butter, softened
3/4 c. all-purpose flour, sifted

1-1/2 c. brown sugar, packed
2 T. cinnamon
1 t. allspice

Spread pecans on a baking sheet. Bake at 350 degrees for 7 to 12 minutes, until toasted, checking often to avoid overbaking. Cool; combine pecans and remaining ingredients. Mix with a fork until crumbs form.

Treat tea-loving friends to a selection of spiced teas, along with fresh lemon wedges and honey.

Favorite Desserts for **Sharing**

Maple Pecan Pie

Elaine Lucas
Runge, TX

My sister gave me this recipe many years ago and it quickly became my husband's favorite pie! I usually serve it for his birthday instead of a cake.

14-oz. can sweetened condensed
  milk
3/4 c. waffle & pancake syrup
2 eggs, beaten

1 c. toasted chopped pecans
9-inch graham cracker crust
Garnish: frozen whipped topping,
  thawed

In a large heavy saucepan, combine condensed milk, syrup and eggs. Bring to a boil over high heat. Reduce heat to medium-low and boil for 5 minutes, stirring constantly. (Be careful, as mixture scorches easily.) Add pecans and mix well. Pour mixture into graham cracker crust. Set aside to cool completely. Cut into wedges and top with whipped topping. Makes 8 servings.

For an easy fall centerpiece, hollow out shiny red apples and tuck tea lights inside. Arrange on a cake stand and surround with greenery...sweet and simple!

Fall Cooking
with Family & Friends

Grandma's Apple Dapple Cake

Tracie Carlson
Richardson, TX

I always knew when fall had arrived, because my grandma was making this spectacularly moist, decadent apple cake with a homey caramel frosting. Wow!

2 c. sugar
1-1/2 c. oil
3 eggs, beaten
2 t. vanilla extract
3 c. all-purpose flour
1 t. salt

1 t. baking soda
1 t. cinnamon
3 c. Granny Smith or Gala apples, peeled, cored and chopped
1 c. chopped walnuts
Optional: whipped cream

In a large bowl, combine sugar, oil, eggs and vanilla. Beat together until light and fluffy; set aside. In another bowl, sift together flour, salt, baking soda and cinnamon. Gradually add flour mixture to sugar mixture; mix well. Fold in apples and nuts; mix thoroughly. Pour batter into a buttered and floured 13"x9" baking pan. Bake at 350 degrees for 45 to 60 minutes, until cake tests done with a toothpick. Remove from oven. Poke cake all over with a knife to allow frosting to penetrate. While cake is still warm, spread Frosting over cake. Cut into squares; top with whipped cream, if desired. Makes 16 servings.

Frosting:

1 c. brown sugar, packed
1 c. light cream

1/2 c. butter, sliced

Mix all ingredients in a small saucepan over medium heat. Cook, stirring often, until mixture comes to a boil. Boil, stirring constantly, for 3 minutes. Let cool for several minutes.

Caramel ice cream topping makes a delightful drizzle over apple desserts...just heat it in the microwave for a few seconds.

Favorite Desserts for Sharing

Autumn Spice Cookies

Courtney Stultz
Weir, KS

These deliciously crisp and spicy cookies are perfect for cooler weather. Grab a cup of milk, tea or coffee and enjoy these with your favorite people!

1/4 c. raw honey
1/4 c. coconut sugar, honey
　or molasses
1/2 c. butter, softened
1 t. vanilla extract
1/4 c. applesauce,
　or 1 egg, beaten

1-1/4 c. all-purpose flour
1/2 t. baking soda
1/2 t. sea salt
1 t. cinnamon
1/4 t. nutmeg
1/4 t. ground cloves

In a bowl, beat together honey, sugar and butter until smooth and fluffy, about 2 minutes. Add vanilla and applesauce or egg; beat until smooth. Add flour, baking soda, salt and spices; beat until combined. Using a large cookie scoop, scoop out dough and place on a parchment paper-lined baking sheet. Gently press cookies flat with the palm of your hand. Bake at 325 degrees for about 10 minutes, until lightly golden. Let cookies cool completely on a wire rack, or they will crumble easily. Makes one dozen.

Getting a head start on your Christmas cookies? Pop up a big bowl of fresh popcorn on baking day. The kids (and you!) will have something tasty to nibble on, saving the nuts and chocolate chips for the cookies.

Fall Cooking
with *Family & Friends*

Marilyn's Scrumptious Butter Pecan Trifle

Marilyn Delph
Cridersville, OH

I created this scrumptious recipe using my late mom's recipe for homemade butterscotch pudding. It has become a favorite at all of our family gatherings.

15-1/4 oz. pkg. butter pecan cake mix
2 16-oz. containers frozen whipped topping, thawed
3/4 c. chopped pecans

Prepare Butterscotch Pudding; set aside to cool. Prepare and bake cake mix as directed on package, using a 13"x9" baking pan. Set aside to cool; cut into one-inch squares. In a large glass trifle bowl, layer 1/3 each of cake squares, pudding and whipped topping. Repeat layers twice, ending with topping. Sprinkle with pecans. Cover and chill until serving time. Makes 12 servings.

Butterscotch Pudding:

2 c. brown sugar, packed
4 egg yolks, beaten
4 c. milk
1/4 c. all-purpose flour
1/4 c. cornstarch
2 t. vanilla extract
1/4 c. butter, sliced

In a large, heavy saucepan over medium heat, combine brown sugar, egg yolks, milk, flour and cornstarch. Whisking constantly, cook until mixture thickens and comes to a boil. Remove from heat; stir in vanilla and butter. Set aside to cool.

Happiness being a dessert so sweet,
May life give you more than you
can ever eat.
–Irish Toast

Favorite Desserts for **Sharing**

Pumpkin Pie Cupcakes

Lori Haines
Johnson City, TN

These yummy cupcakes are excellent to make ahead and freeze. Pull out exactly how many you need, about an hour before you want to serve. Perfect for unexpected guests, a small snack or a make-ahead dessert. This will create the illusion that you've been working hard all day!

18-1/4 oz. pkg. spice cake mix
15-oz. can pumpkin, divided
2 t. pumpkin pie spice, divided
8-oz. pkg. cream cheese
1 c. powdered sugar
1/2 c. sugar
2 t. vanilla extract
8-oz. container frozen whipped
   topping, thawed

In a large bowl, prepare cake mix as package directs. Add 1/2 can pumpkin and one teaspoon spice to batter. Beat with an electric mixer on medium speed for 2 minutes, or until smooth. Divide batter evenly among 24 paper-lined muffin cups. Bake at 350 degrees for 13 minutes. Immediately remove cupcakes from pan; cover with plastic wrap and let cool. For frosting, in a large bowl, combine cream cheese, sugars, vanilla and remaining spice; beat until smooth. Fold in whipped topping and remaining pumpkin. Spoon frosting into a one-gallon plastic zipping bag. Snip off a small hole in one corner; squirt a generous amount onto each cupcake. Store cupcakes in an airtight container; refrigerate or freeze. Makes 2 dozen.

Make a delicious buffet even more inviting! Set a variety of cake and dessert stands on the table to create different levels. Fill with desserts...stand back and wait for the ooh's and aah's!

Fall Cooking
with Family & Friends

Vintage Cherry-Coconut-Pecan Bars

Debbie Adkins
Nicholasville, KY

I got this wonderful recipe about 30 years ago from my husband's Uncle Fred and it's one of the best I've ever had. It's great for taking to parties, because it doesn't need to be refrigerated.

4 eggs, lightly beaten
2 c. sugar
1/2 c. all-purpose flour
1 t. baking powder
1/2 t. salt

2 t. vanilla extract
1-1/2 c. coarsely chopped pecans
1 c. sweetened flaked coconut
1 c. maraschino cherries, drained
 and quartered

Prepare and bake Crust. Meanwhile, in a large bowl, whisk together eggs and sugar until well mixed. Add remaining ingredients and stir well. When crust is finished baking, spread egg mixture evenly over crust. Bake at 350 degrees for about 25 minutes. Cool; cut into squares. Store at room temperature in an airtight container. Makes 3 dozen.

Crust:

2 c. all-purpose flour
1 c. butter, room temperature

6 T. powdered sugar

Combine flour, butter and powdered sugar; stir until well mixed. Pat firmly into the bottom of an aluminum foil-lined 13"x9" baking pan. Bake at 350 degrees for 20 to 25 minutes, until pale and very lightly golden (not brown).

Still have fun-size chocolate candy bars left over from Halloween?
Use them to make deluxe s'mores...yummy!

Favorite Desserts
for **Sharing**

Roly-Polys

Cassie Hooker
La Porte, TX

This recipe was in the first cookbook I ever received as a child. These cookies were the very first cookies I ever learned to bake. They take me back to my childhood days, when Mom and I would bake them together. I guess you could say this was when I developed my love for baking!

1 c. shortening
1-1/2 c. plus 2 T. sugar, divided
2 eggs, beaten
2-3/4 c. all-purpose flour
2 t. cream of tartar
1 t. baking soda
1/8 t. salt
2 t. cinnamon

Combine shortening, 1-1/2 cups sugar and eggs in a large bowl; mix well. Add flour, cream of tartar, baking soda and salt; mix together well. In a small bowl, combine cinnamon and remaining sugar. Roll dough into small balls and dip into cinnamon-sugar mixture. Place on lightly greased baking sheets. Bake at 350 degrees for 8 to 10 minutes. Makes 2 dozen.

There is always something for
which to be thankful.
–Charles Dickens

Fall Cooking
with *Family & Friends*

Family Favorite Fruit Pizza

Elizabeth Langenegger
Metairie, LA

My mom and grandma have made this dessert for 40 years.
I always requested it on my birthday instead of a cake. If you like,
save time by using a store-bought pie crust.

1/2 c. shortening
1-1/2 c. all-purpose flour
5 to 6 T. water
1/8 t. salt
8-oz. pkg. cream cheese,
  softened

1/4 c. sugar
8-oz. container frozen whipped
  topping, thawed
Garnish: sliced strawberries,
  kiwi fruit, bananas,
  mandarin oranges

In a bowl, combine shortening, flour, water and salt; mix together until dough is formed. Spread dough on an ungreased 12" round pizza pan. Bake at 425 degrees for 10 to 15 minutes. Prepare Glaze while crust is baking; set aside to cool. Meanwhile, beat together cream cheese and sugar; spread over crust. Spread a layer of whipped topping over cream cheese mixture. Arrange strawberries in a row around outer edge, then a row of bananas, then a row of kiwi, then a row of oranges. Repeat until entire surface is covered to the center. Spread cooled Glaze over fruit. To serve, cut into wedges. Serves 6 to 8.

Glaze:

3/4 c. water
1/2 c. orange juice
1/4 c. lemon juice

1/2 c. sugar
2 T. cornstarch

Combine all ingredients in a saucepan. Cook and stir over low heat until thickened and sugar is dissolved. Let cool.

Mom's vintage Thanksgiving turkey platter is perfect for heaping with a variety of tasty cookies.

Favorite Desserts for **Sharing**

Famous Oatmeal Cookies

Leona Krivda
Belle Vernon, PA

We have been making this same cookie recipe in my family for years. Sometimes we tweak it and add some white chocolate chips and dried cranberries. When I make these cookies, I usually have to make a triple batch, because this is the one and only cookie at my house that no one can stay out of!

3/4 c. shortening
1 c. brown sugar, packed
1/2 c. sugar
1 egg, beaten
1/4 c. water
1 t. vanilla extract

3 c. rolled oats, uncooked
1 c. all-purpose flour
1/2 t. baking soda
1 t. salt
1 c. chopped walnuts or pecans

In a large bowl, beat together shortening, sugars, egg, water and vanilla until creamy; set aside. In another bowl, whisk together oats, flour, baking soda and salt. Slowly add oat mixture to shortening mixture; stir well. Fold in nuts. Drop dough by teaspoonfuls onto greased baking sheets. Bake at 350 degrees for 10 to 12 minutes. Cool on wire racks. Makes 5 to 5-1/2 dozen.

The frost is on the pumpkin! For an elegant yet easy fall centerpiece, spray a pumpkin lightly with spray adhesive and sprinkle with clear glitter. Set the pumpkin on a cake stand and cover with a clear glass dome.

Fall Cooking
with Family & Friends

Something Special Popcorn

Lynda Hart
Bluffdale, UT

I like to make this special popcorn for Halloween and Christmas.
You may wish to make two batches...it disappears in the blink of
an eye! Ribbon coconut is good in this, and toasted coconut adds a
special flavor.

16 c. popped popcorn
1 c. pecan halves
1 c. whole almonds
1 c. walnut halves
1 c. shredded coconut

1 c. butter, sliced
1-1/3 c. sugar
1/2 c. corn syrup
1/2 t. vanilla extract
1/2 t. cinnamon

Place popcorn in a large heat-proof bowl; remove any unpopped
kernels. Add nuts and coconut; set aside. In a heavy saucepan over
medium-high heat, combine butter, sugar and corn syrup. Bring to a
boil; boil for exactly one minute. Add vanilla and cinnamon; stir well.
Pour butter mixture over popcorn mixture; mix well to coat. Spread out
on a parchment paper-lined baking sheet to cool. Store in an airtight
container. Makes 20 cups.

Create a sweet back-to-school display on the mantel with
children's alphabet blocks, slate chalkboards, old-fashioned
school books and vintage tin lunch pails. Don't forget
a shiny apple for the teacher!

Favorite Desserts
for Sharing

Fall Candy Mix

Beckie Apple
Grannis, AR

This simple candy mix brings back lots of fond memories. It was a quick fix for little masked ghosts, goblins, witches and clowns at Halloween. I would mix it up and then put in snack-size bags. It's still popular today.

2 lbs. candy corn
1 lb. salted peanuts

1 lb. candy-coated chocolate
  candies

Combine all ingredients in a large bowl; mix well. Fill snack-size bags for easy serving. Serves 10 to 12.

Fall Yummies

Donna Wilson
Maryville, TN

I love to make these candies to share with my family & friends. They're easy to put together. I also like to pour this into holiday candy molds for a really cute presentation. Very nice for parties!

8-oz. pkg. semi-sweet baking
  chocolate, chopped

1/2 c. chopped almonds
1/2 c. dried cranberries

Microwave chocolate in a microwave-safe bowl on high for 30 seconds; stir. Microwave for 30 seconds more; stir. Continue heating in 10-second increments, until melted. Stir in almonds and cranberries; drop by teaspoonfuls onto wax paper. Let set for 30 minutes or so. If desired, refrigerate to set up quicker. Serves 10.

Look for mini enamelware pails in bright home-team colors... they're perfect for filling with sweets and treats.

Fall Cooking
with *Family & Friends*

Taffy Apple Bundt Cake

Melody Taynor
Everett, WA

We love our Washington state apples! This is a scrumptious cake to make with them that's just perfect for all those special fall occasions. If you don't have a Bundt® pan, a 13"x9" baking pan can be used. Bake for 75 to 80 minutes.

1-1/2 c. butter, softened
4-1/2 c. powdered sugar
1 T. vanilla extract
6 eggs
3-1/4 c. all-purpose flour
2 t. cinnamon
1 t. allspice

16 caramels, unwrapped and
   cut into 8 pieces each
1-1/2 c. tart baking apples,
   peeled, cored and diced
Optional: vanilla ice cream,
   caramel topping

In a large bowl, with an electric mixer on medium speed, beat together butter, powdered sugar and vanilla until light and fluffy. Add eggs, one at a time, beating well after each. Gradually add flour and spices to egg mixture. Beat on low speed until thoroughly combined. Fold in caramels and apples. Pour batter into a greased 10" Bundt® pan. Bake at 325 degrees for 85 to 90 minutes, until a toothpick inserted near the center tests clean. Set pan on a wire rack and cool for 15 minutes. Turn out onto a serving platter. Serve warm or cool, garnished as desired. Serves 12.

Garnish a Bundt® cake with a sparkling bunch of sugared grapes... so pretty! Just brush grapes with a thin mixture of meringue powder and water, roll in fine sugar and let dry.

Favorite Desserts for Sharing

Giant Chocolate Chip Cookie

Tina Wright
Atlanta, GA

My son asks for this giant cookie as his birthday cake. He likes it so much that when his football team won the championship, he asked me to make a special cookie decorated for the celebration. I've even given it as a gift, tucked into a new pizza box from a nearby pizza shop.

1 c. butter, softened	1 t. baking soda
3/4 c. brown sugar, packed	1 t. salt
3/4 c. sugar	2 c. semi-sweet chocolate chips
1 t. vanilla extract	1 c. chopped walnuts
2 eggs	Optional: frosting, candy
2-1/4 c. all-purpose flour	sprinkles

In a large bowl, with an electric mixer on medium speed, beat together butter, sugars and vanilla until light and fluffy. Add eggs, one at a time, beating well. Gradually add flour, baking soda and salt, beating until well blended. Stir in chocolate chips and nuts. Spread dough in a greased 14" round pizza pan. Bake at 375 degrees for 20 to 25 minutes. Set pan on a wire rack to cool. Decorate as desired; cut into wedges or squares to serve. Makes 16 servings.

If the grandparents live out of town, why not invite an older neighbor or friend of the family to join you and the kids in a cookie baking day? You're sure to have fun together.

Fall Cooking
with *Family & Friends*

Pumpkin-Cranberry Bread
Annette Ceravolo
Hoover, AL

This has become a family favorite for the holidays. I start baking several loaves before Thanksgiving, so I'll have enough to give to relatives as they leave the house after our big day together.

2-1/4 c. all-purpose flour
1 T. pumpkin pie spice
2 t. baking powder
1/2 t. salt
2 eggs

1-1/2 to 2 c. sugar
1/2 c. canola oil
15-oz. can pumpkin
1 c. dried cranberries
1/2 c. chopped walnuts

Combine flour, spice, baking powder and salt in a large bowl; mix well and set aside. Beat eggs in a separate bowl. Add sugar, oil and pumpkin; mix well. Stir flour mixture into pumpkin mixture. Add cranberries and walnuts; mix thoroughly. Spoon batter into 2 greased and floured 9"x5" loaf pans. Bake at 350 degrees for 55 minutes, or until a wooden toothpick inserted in center comes out clean. Let cool in pans for 20 minutes. Turn out loaves; cool completely on wire rack. Makes 2 loaves.

A gift of homemade quick bread is always welcome...it can even
be made one to 2 months ahead and frozen. To keep it oven-fresh,
let the bread cool completely before wrapping first in aluminum
foil, then in plastic wrap.

Favorite Desserts for **Sharing**

Mom's Banana Bread

Kimberly Redeker
Savoy, IL

A delicious after-school snack. My mom always made this bread when the bananas were starting to turn. She always added nuts, but once I had her substitute chocolate chips when she was making it for me. Now it's Dad's favorite that way, too!

1/2 c. butter
1 c. sugar
2 eggs, beaten
2-1/2 c. all-purpose flour

1 t. baking powder
1 t. baking soda
3 over-ripe bananas, mashed
1 c. semi-sweet chocolate chips

Blend butter and sugar in a large bowl; stir in eggs and set aside. In another bowl, mix flour, baking powder and baking soda. Gradually add flour mixture to egg mixture; stir well. Add bananas and mix well; fold in chocolate chips. Pour batter into a greased 9"x5" loaf pan. Bake at 350 degrees for about one hour, testing for doneness with a toothpick. May also divide batter among 3 greased mini loaf pans; bake at 350 degrees for about 45 minutes. Makes one regular loaf or 3 mini loaves.

Store over-ripe and browned bananas in the freezer until you have enough for yummy banana bread. They'll keep for about 2 to 3 months!

INDEX

INDEX

INDEX

Find Gooseberry Patch
wherever you are!

www.gooseberrypatch.com

Email

Blog

You Tube

Call us toll-free at 1·800·854·6673

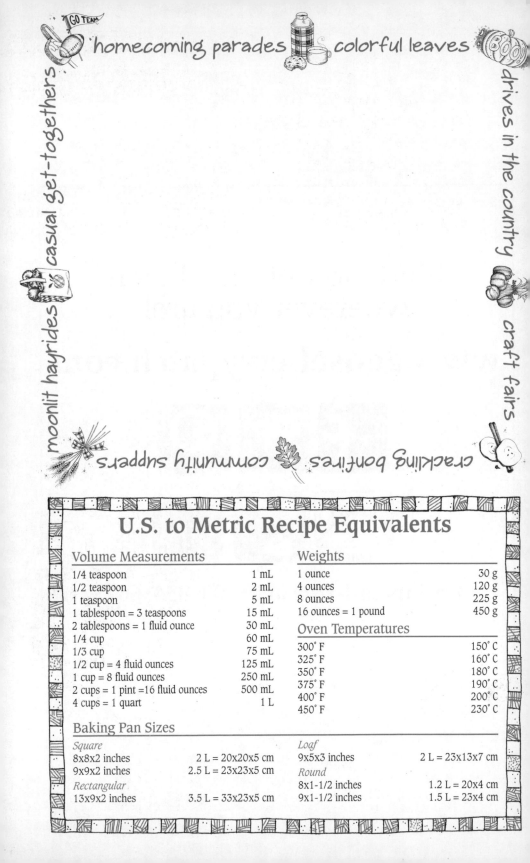

homecoming parades colorful leaves

drives in the country

craft fairs

casual get-togethers

moonlit hayrides

crackling bonfires community suppers

U.S. to Metric Recipe Equivalents

Volume Measurements

1/4 teaspoon	1 mL
1/2 teaspoon	2 mL
1 teaspoon	5 mL
1 tablespoon = 3 teaspoons	15 mL
2 tablespoons = 1 fluid ounce	30 mL
1/4 cup	60 mL
1/3 cup	75 mL
1/2 cup = 4 fluid ounces	125 mL
1 cup = 8 fluid ounces	250 mL
2 cups = 1 pint =16 fluid ounces	500 mL
4 cups = 1 quart	1 L

Weights

1 ounce	30 g
4 ounces	120 g
8 ounces	225 g
16 ounces = 1 pound	450 g

Oven Temperatures

300° F	150° C
325° F	160° C
350° F	180° C
375° F	190° C
400° F	200° C
450° F	230° C

Baking Pan Sizes

Square		Loaf	
8x8x2 inches	2 L = 20x20x5 cm	9x5x3 inches	2 L = 23x13x7 cm
9x9x2 inches	2.5 L = 23x23x5 cm	Round	
Rectangular		8x1-1/2 inches	1.2 L = 20x4 cm
13x9x2 inches	3.5 L = 33x23x5 cm	9x1-1/2 inches	1.5 L = 23x4 cm